flo

i stand up you

i need you

to gether, we'll make
it to the end

never give up !

love us
ps. 91

# STRUGGLING FOR WHOLENESS

Books by Ann Kiemel Anderson

*Hi! I'm Ann*
*I'm Out to Change My World*
*I Love the Word Impossible*
*It's Incredible!*
*Yes*
*I'm Celebrating*
*I'm Running to Win*
*I Gave God Time*
*Taste of Tears, Touch of God*

Audio Cassettes by Jan Kiemel Ream

*A Healthy Family*
*Woman to Woman: Understanding Your Sexuality*
*A Life Full of Needs*
*Journey Toward Wholeness*

# STRUGGLING
## *for Wholeness*

*Ann Kiemel Anderson*
*and*
*Jan Kiemel Ream*

A Division of Thomas Nelson Publishers
Nashville • Atlanta • Camden • New York

Published in Nashville, Tennessee, by Oliver-Nelson Books, a division of Thomas Nelson, Inc., Publishers, and distributed in Canada by Lawson Falle, Ltd., Cambridge, On-
tario.

Scripture quotations are from the NEW KING JAMES VERSION. Copyright © 1979,
1980, 1982, Thomas Nelson Inc., Publishers.

The persons identified as "clients" represent a composite of Jan Kiemel Ream's practice,
and no one individual is portrayed in this volume.

Printed in the United States of America.

**Library of Congress Cataloging-in-Publication Data**

Anderson, Ann Kiemel.
  Struggling for wholeness.

  1. Women—United States—Psychology—Case studies.
2. Identity (Psychology)—Case studies. 3. Self-
actualization (Psychology)—Case studies. 4. Twins—
Psychology—Case studies. I. Ream, Jan Kiemel,
1945-        II. Title.
HQ1206.A53    1986      155.6'33      85-31085
ISBN 9-8407-9042-2
3 4 5 6 7 8 9 10 11 12 13 14 15 16 17 18 19 20—90 89 88 87 86

to our small sons

brock
christian
nash
taylor
tre


with such love
...and a quiet prayer that they may be
brave enough...& real enough...
to seek for wholeness, too.

# Contents

# Foreword

You are going to have fun with this book. You will laugh and cry and say to yourself, "I can't believe she said that." This is a book written by two women, twins, who are struggling every day to become whole people.

Jan and Ann, daughters of an "old-time" evangelical minister, have had multifaceted careers. They are both married with children. Ann's are adopted—she's still hoping for a normal pregnancy of her own. The husbands are successful businessmen who challenge their wives to be all they can be in life. Ann has written several books and has talked to hundreds of thousands of people in conventions across the globe. Jan is a practicing marriage and family therapist who lectures across the country when her clients let her out of the office.

Both women have a unique gift: a disarming honesty and transparency which allows them to identify with the struggles, pain, and joy—in fact, all the nitty-gritty issues—of being a whole person in these demanding times. In this book they will confront you with their insights on friendships, sexuality, conflict, and a variety of other topics challenging women today.

THE PUBLISHER

# Opening

  this is our story of wholeness. of not arriving there, but of moving in that direction. of reaching out & beginning to really grasp it.

  jan & i are sitting in a beautiful condo loaned to us by generous people, in the tetons of jackson hole, wyoming. it seems too idyllic & perfect to write in this atmosphere....but we felt we should bring our babies. jan's is seven months—mine is nine months. to leave them with loving people during the day, & pick them up each evening & spend time with them. tuck them into cribs ourselves. feed them. cuddle them & rock them. make sure they are not insecure while we try to tell the world about feeling whole & secure.

  that *was* our idea. it seemed perfect. however, before we left idaho falls ( jan & baby christian flew in there from cleveland), both babies were so fussy & abnormal we decided they should be checked. stopping at the family emergency center, we discovered they both had serious ear infections, temperatures, congestion. thus, antibiotics, triaminic, tylenol. sobbing...each of them before we arrived in jackson. it was after dark when we arrived. unloading the *little* rent-a-car in sub-zero weather, pitch-dark of night, up stairs, 22-lb. little chunks under our arms. couldn't get the heat going. no sheets. no soap. the refrigerator not working. (the condo lenders, of course, not aware of these problems!)

  we ended up in one bedroom that had heat. one double bed. two babies & two adults squeezed together. christian (jan's) wheezing & coughing & restless. which would trigger taylor. one would fall asleep & 30 minutes later the other, in pain, would awaken & fuss. then they would both be awake. crying.

  the milk for bottles outside the door to stay cold. the

milk freezing. the clock radio by the bed going off at 4:30 A.M. just as we had finally *all* dropped into sleep.

well…it's "tomorrow." the heat is finally working in the condominium. the refrigerator humming. a telephone retrieved & plugged in to give us touch with the outside world. the babies, wide-eyed & dazed, left sitting on the floor of what is supposed to be "the best" child-care center. jan & i have had eggs & bacon for breakfast to try & revive our worn-out state. we sit here, paper & pens, trying to share with you some thread of truth that will lead you on your way. neither of us feels whole enough today to really help you—but…

we believe in this story. it is our own. from small, skinny, plain, struggling children, twin daughters of a fundamentalist minister, to 39-year-old women. from building our lives around perfection for the most part. the warped concept that if we can somehow be flawless, unscathed, very-together people, the world & God will love us & then we can be ourselves…to understanding that absolutely no one ever achieves that, & is unstable if they try. to knowing that wholeness…seeing the pluses & negatives…the strengths & weaknesses…accepting both…blending both…growing from & sharing both…well, this is the secret to deep, abiding joy & contentment.

we are back in jackson hole where i honeymooned four years ago, & began the greatest encounter with myself. it was the beginning of the brutal stripping that led me to my truest self. jan & her husband, tom, shared a week of that honeymoon here with us, & it was at that point jan decided, whatever the cost, to break away from her sense of deep inferiority when she compared herself with me, & find her own great worth.

with love & care, here in jackson hole, we share with you what we have learned. praying you can share the journey, too, & find healing.

ANN KIEMEL ANDERSON

# 1.
# Struggling to Find Our Special Place

## ann

my sister, jan, & i are doing this book together. it is her first, my tenth. she's been mother, wife, years before i met will or got taylor. & a professional psychologist with hundreds of clients & other therapists helping her. she has flown in to various places & helped me to write almost all of my books. reminded me of experiences. created concepts. critiqued my pages but this is her first experience at sharing the joy & pain of baring one's soul on paper for others to read.

for me, it's a new place in allowing her to do this. being identical twins, we grew up with such singleness of identity.

"here come the twins."

as if we were not two people. individuals. separate. different, unique. so as we got older, we developed our own ways of expressing our personalities to the world. i was the leader, jan, the follower. i the speaker & writer. jan, the wife, mother, psychologist. we have never, until four years ago when i married, crossed over into each other's worlds. they were sacred. they gave us each our own special place, not only with the world, but with each other.

today, as we write, i am letting jan become a part of, & own a place that, for us, has just been mine. i think i am ready for that. excited. except, after reading some of the pages she's written, & how good they are, i feel a little uncertain. what if she is really better at this than i've ever been? what if you begin

*Editor's note:* Ann & Jan have written about events and feelings according to subject rather than according to the order in which experiences and thoughts occurred.

to want her stuff more than mine? to open myself to this…to take that risk…to allow her to express her full circle of gifts & feelings…is a part of my becoming more whole.

to cheer her on. to be actually thrilled & elated if her writing is better received than mine. to want her to succeed as much as i long to be reassured that i have something to offer you. to not have to compete on a level that says unless i have some kind of edge, there will be tension. not to seem to be decent on the outside but hurt & defensive & threatened on the inside.

ironically, jan has owned the uniqueness of being married, having a husband. becoming pregnant (our greatest, deepest, childhood dream). having beautiful & extraordinary (we think) children. when i married will four years ago, she faced her greatest challenge in being whole. i had crossed into her territory. she thought maybe i would be a better wife, probably. now, i would have children, & be a better mother. what she owned as most valuable & unique in her relationship with me was having to be shared. given away.

though i had terrible infertility problems…infections …miscarriages…we did adopt taylor as a newborn. what a child! what a gift. yet, jan still had the pregnancies, the deliveries, of her & tom's own creations. however, two weeks ago, i learned i am pregnant. they seem healthy. as if i will carry these babies full term. jan, in her own right, is no longer holding something as just hers. it is a new place in her development of wholeness. deep down inside, i have feared other people doing better than i. being compared & falling short. not being as good as. maybe there is a part of me that is terrified that if, in some way, i am not better than someone else in some area, then you will not value me. i will be lost. it is so small of me, isn't it!

always, i seem to need things that make me feel special. i valued my thin body, because so many battle weight. because it has made up for the fact that i don't have the most flawless, beautiful skin. do you understand?

one night before Christmas, will & i were invited to a gourmet club hors d'oeuvres party. i did not know anyone. will can talk to anyone about almost anything. he is so well read. so comfortable about himself. at least he seems to be. a very attractive woman was introduced to me. a physician in joint practice with her husband. a mother of four or five children. a skier. so productive & seemingly self-assured. i was quietly overwhelmed. the only thing i could think of to say, after casual informalities were covered, was "i am a writer." it still seemed insignificant to her roster of accomplishments, but it was better than nothing. of course, i worked at sounding low-key & casual, but i was sure to somehow try & let her know i, too, was important.

two days later, i wrote her:

dear sally—it was so special meeting you. you are amazing & profound. you put so much into life. please forgive me for trying to impress you with something that was mine. as if my value were wrapped up in achieving something you might value. as if i had to tell you. to let you know. there is so much more for me to learn.

she became my baby's doctor. my friend. i continue to like her thoroughly, & respect her & her husband immensely. i know, however, that for wholeness i must let jan experience *every* avenue of creative accomplishment possible. i must cheer & root for & run beside her, giving all the support & help she needs. she must do the same for me. i do not have to own things all by myself. or be better than. or make grand statements to the "sallys" at parties. i have worth. my worth comes from God. but you also help develop it. as we each encourage the other in it, the sunrise will spread across the sky. the warmth & laughter. the peace. the joy.

this sounds as if i just walked into this seemingly simple, uncomplicated place. that it was natural for me. it does make me sound so *nice*. so together.

but only by process...years & years of struggle ...failure...growth am i arriving at this attitude. through tremendous fear. an almost unimaginable sense of inferiority. determinedly forcing my pain to the front where i could look at it & deal with it. jan has been my partner. my therapist. my friend. my person to tell all my secrets to. to unfold my greatest fears before. we are walking this journey together. & my guess is that many of you readers are too.

# Jan

I think the first moment in my entire life that I felt God really loved me as much as Ann was when I delivered my first son, Tre. Feeling as I did about myself, very inferior, and knowing all my quirks and flaws and Tom's, too. I was amazed as I looked down at this perfect, beautiful baby. While I hadn't written best-selling books or traveled the world over as a greatly sought-after lecturer, as Ann had, I had conceived, carried, and delivered a baby. I remember the ecstatic joy at 6 A.M. in the hospital when they rolled in that tiny basket marked BABY REAM for his early morning feeding. And the intense pleasure of leaving him with my mother at twelve days of age, for the first time, and going to a bridal shower. Not as "Jan Ream," but as "Jan Ream—*Mother*." I was a real mother. Most of my childhood years with Ann were spent playing "mothers" and "wives" and now I really was one.

I was in a therapy session when the secretary buzzed my office and told me Dr. Adams was on the phone. I knew he was going to tell me the results of my pregnancy test. It surely couldn't be positive. That would have been too good to be true. "Jan, your test was positive." No words in the human language could express the wonder and awe of those words. It was as if I was the only woman in the entire world to ever hear them. Regardless of how many more times a woman conceives and delivers, there is something unique about that first experience, that which we have read about, heard about, learned about, but finally are experiencing for the first time, that helps it stand out like neon lights.

16

I thought I always wanted Ann to be a wife and mother with me. We could take great trips together and live out our childhood games of playing house. When Ann married Will Anderson, it brought with it the most traumatic pain I had ever felt. It was during their honeymoon when I finally realized the bottom of my pain lay in the fact that after living side by side with her all of my life, she had seemingly always beaten me in any task we set out to conquer. The only competition I had not had with her—nor had somehow come in a hair behind—was that of being a wife and mother. But now that she was entering those two turfs she would certainly supersede me again. I used to feel great anger at God for making me so inferior. How ever could He keep helping her gain so much worth and recognition and leave me standing by smiling, so no one would know how badly I felt—and feel sorry for me. I never wanted to be better than Ann, only *as good as.*

When I finally surrendered my fear to God and determined that whatever it took, I would learn to like myself, I soon began to realize marriage for Ann only brought us closer. She used to say to me long before she married Will, "I wouldn't put up with that in Tom." Usually, I would feel *she's probably right.* I saw her as always being more right than me (or anyone else in the entire world for that matter!). Now that she is married she reports back to me she has had to eat much of her advice to me on marriage. What a comfort. So I wasn't as far off the track as I had felt. Yahoo! A new camaraderie began to take place. The more of life we can all experience together that is somewhat similar, the closer we are drawn to each other—the greater we are able to identify and feel empathy. I have given that advice to many a client and understand it very well intellectually. However, I am saddened to say that as excited and thrilled as I was over her pregnancy, there was a bit of pain in me.

The part of me Ann has admired the most I think is my motherhood. Now I'm afraid she will not value me nearly as much because she is going to discover what only before had been mystique. Will I have any part of me that is really special to her? It is a strange feeling to stand back and watch her tummy grow, and relinquish to her the enormous pride and pleasure I myself felt and that she had so admired about me. I hate the part of me that resists at moments being excited with her and telling her how beautiful she looks.

For years I denied that I ever competed with Ann. But today I ashamedly admit that the feelings are there. In reality, if women were honest, all would confess to it. We just so hate to talk about it.

I like so much what Ann just said though, "forcing my pain to the front where I could look at it and deal with it." I don't think we ever get rid of the struggle and pain that comes from unhealthy competing. My needing to be better than you so I can maintain my worth. Rather I think our freedom comes when we can confess it. When we confess it, we are able to simply say: It is there...and I don't like it. I know it shouldn't be there. Wholeness is most evident when I can let you succeed. Join my turf. My worth is not wrapped up in being better. When you, by some spark of fate, land on my turf, we will be able to see both the positives and negatives of the experience and join each other more deeply and intimately than ever before.

I always know when I'm being too small to share your joy. I can feel it inside. It robs me of sunshine and laughter and peace. It helps always for me to confess it to whomever I'm struggling with.

One of the greatest tasks of finding wholeness is relinquishment—giving to you what I want to keep for myself. Each time I let go and give what I want to hang onto, I lose a little bit more of the fear that keeps me crippled. I gain a more realistic view of life and no longer have to remain trapped and imprisoned by my distorted pictures.

Ann and Will's Taylor, nine months (their first), is a handsome, strong, bright child. I see Ann trying to mother "exactly right" and I remember how I felt about Tre. I felt he was brighter and better behaved than any other baby his age. I used to look at other parents critically, at times wishing I could show them a better way. At moments fear creeps inside me, without my permission, and tries to suggest again Ann is in fact going to be a better mother. I watch her and say, "Did I do all those things, too?" Now that Tre is eight, and we've added Nash (five years) and now Christian (seven months), I've run into some snags. My children don't always:

- look into people's eyes when they're talked to
- get billed as the finest students their teachers ever taught

In fact, I've stumbled away from more than one parent-teacher conference muttering, "Where have I already gone wrong as a mother?"

I've run into some potholes. Being a mother isn't as easy as it looked when I was a single schoolteacher with lots of available advice to any parent who was interested enough to ask. I sometimes gave it to those who didn't ask. Some days I'm not even convinced I should have become a mother. It's not that my children aren't incredibly wonderful. They are. But I keep running into myself in them and I admit I'm frightened by what I see. Ann, with her nine month old, hasn't experienced the pain and joy of one child succeeding while the other child stands by feeling inferior. I know that pain well. Or of the wrenching, watching a four-year-old in emotional pain burst into tears and express, "Only Nash [then the new baby] is good. I'm not good anymore." I have a great friend who says, "I would have gone through life thinking I was a wonderful person if I had never had a child."

In my head I know Ann will experience this gray side of mothering—the part you can't seem to make perfect in spite of how hard you try. When she does, I think I will find new freedom from fear, new wholeness. I will once again have the opportunity to realize a clearer picture of what life really is. I will be able to be less fearful of myself. I'm most afraid of myself in those moments, you know. Afraid that wrapped up in this body and person of me, Jan Ream, I will only amount to the totally unknown insignificant person I felt I was as a child.

All of our life people have compared us. They would get an inch from our faces and try to find a bump or freckle that would distinguish us. They were probably looking for differences. I felt they were seeing who was "better." When someone in my audiences comes up and says, "I enjoy hearing you speak more," it is never a compliment to either of us. Why can't they find something positive about both our styles and appreciate the fact we *are* different? A great deal of insecurity in this world comes from the tendency to compare ourselves as better or worse, brighter or dumber, fatter or skinnier. We have trouble seeing just ourselves as a packaged entity. We compare ourselves with others and others with ourselves. We end up viewing ourselves as above or below those around us.

We move closer to wholeness when we are able to see the genius in all of us.

One New Year's Eve we were with a wonderful family and their three grown sons. The father had us each express to everyone in the circle what we liked the most about them. It was such a great, reinforcing experience. I loved hearing seven wonderful things about myself. I was amazed by what they saw in me that I didn't see. And it was exhilarating to be healthy and whole enough to be able to celebrate someone else's great strengths.

Tre, eight years, and Nash, five years, were in the circle. Nash's legs kicking over the side of a chair, and Tre fidgeting with a stick for the fire. They had never been in a group like this before. I admit I was more focused in on them than myself. Would they sit still through this? Would the people in the group realize they were "people," too, and affirm them? What I was anxiously afraid of happened—a couple of people bypassed both children when they came to them and went on to the next adult. I think I know my little sons. They revealed their stinging awareness that they were passed as nonentities by squirming a little extra or taking a tongue and licking the full circumference of their little mouths. I couldn't *wait* for my turn.

"Nash, you make me laugh and smile all over. You say things to Mommy that leave me speechless for minutes. Like the day driving home from school I looked at your big, droopy eyes and said, 'Honey, you're tired.' You retorted, 'I'm not. How can you say that? You don't have X-ray vision. You can't read my mind. Not even I have X-ray vision. I don't even know if I'm tired.' "

Nash looked right at me and those magical, brown eyes sparkled like diamonds. He was able to capture a uniqueness in himself.

I looked at Tre, my almost-eight-year-old, "Tre Ream, my firstborn son, you are able to see and feel things many adults can't seem to perceive. I've had some of my greatest talks with you. As powerful and moving as with any adult I've ever known." Tears trickled down my cheeks.

In that moment I was able to reveal to the group something dynamic about a somewhat shy, reserved child they might have missed. The group beautifully began to respond more personally to him.

My mother used to say to Ann and me, "I could put you both in a paper bag and shake it, and you'd both come out equal." I was always so comforted by that. I wish the rest of the world could have seen and responded to me that way.

Ann and I were co-speakers at a meeting a few months past. We walked into the hotel lobby side by side up to the desk. The woman behind the desk expecting both of us looked straight at Ann and said, "Ann Kiemel, I can't believe you're here. We're so excited to have you." She never looked in my direction or acknowledged me. I spent years turning the burning pain of feeling not as special inward and finding a bathroom to weep out my pain. Today it angers me. I know I'm worth more than that.

I have never aspired to write a book. I get almost sick before I write a letter. Ann was the writer of the family. It's more incredulous to me than it could possibly be to anyone that I am able to sit here and pen a paragraph. I'm Ann's greatest fan. I laugh and weep as I read her books. When I need a pickup, I go to the shelf for an Ann Kiemel book, and by the time I've finished reading, I'm out to change the world, too.

I hope you don't compare our writing. I will always appreciate her writing more but I'm learning to say, "Mine is just different." I hope you will say that, too!

There's a genius in each of you, in your mates, in each of your children. Find it. Celebrate it. Capitalize on it. As Bill and Gloria Gaither say, "You are someone special. The only one of your kind."

# 2.
# Getting With It Physically
## Jan

I'm not sure we ever totally at all times can learn to love and accept our bodies. Every three to five months I go to my hairdresser and get the finest body perm you can get. My hair stays full and healthy looking. I think I'd eat cold cereal for months to afford one if I ran into financial stress. For years I teased my hair, feeling my head was too small. One of the greatest risks I ever took was when I changed my hairstyle a few years ago. I not only teased my hair up big (my little sons saw a picture and groaned in disbelief ), but I also wore a hairpiece under the top part of my hair to add even more body and height. The style of teasing had long begun to fade in the world of fashion, but *I* was still clinging to it. I was paralyzed even with the thought of facing life without my hairpiece. I do remember the day I felt inspired (by God, I felt) to get a new hairdo. I threw away my hairpiece. I told Tom I wanted to have a burial service for it. It had played such a big part in my physical identity for so long. I liked my new style. So did others. It felt as if I'd lost a hundred pounds off the top of my head. I liked me *so* much better when I came up with a hairstyle that was becoming to me and "in."

I have found a combination of makeup that I like on my face. It gives me a tanned look—something I've always strived for since Hawaii. I'm amused when people stop me and ask where did I go to get such a nice tan. A little bit embarrassed I say, "out of a bottle." I even keep a bottle of tanning lotion on the shelf for my arms if I'm wearing something in the winter that exposes the white skin I've always struggled over. When I get to heaven (I'm planning to go), I want God to give me beautiful flawless, olive skin. Would you be shocked if I told you I married a man with olive skin?

Most people have some physical attribute they'd like to change. I have a male client who says he's a "teeth" man. He struggles with his teeth, and so is looking for a female who must have nice teeth among other notable qualities.

I had a client who said, "I hate my nose. I know where it came from. I have a grandfather with a nose just like it." I suggested he consider a nose job. If there is some part of your physical body you hate and can change and bring improvement through some medical treatment, I encourage it.

A dermatologist years ago gave Ann and me a little bottle of acid with strict instructions of how to use it (after he became exhausted with us coming in for him to remove more freckles!).

Maybe once every two years we get together and go through the grueling process of burning off a few more freckles that determine to keep surfacing and threaten our sense of well-being. My husband, like Will, says, "I love your freckles. I wouldn't want you to have skin without them." When he and I on a rare occasion go shopping together, he inevitably pulls a backless dress off the rack and says to the clerk, "I would love my wife to wear things like this, but she has freckles on her back," and I could kill him! Will says, "I have never met a person with freckles who isn't smart." (We still feel better if we can rid ourselves of as many as possible!)

Changing your nose or burning off freckles will probably not make others like you better, but it will most likely help you like yourself better. A good self-concept is not just loving "all of you," of seeing no flaws in yourself. Rather it is acknowledging both the strong and the weak and wrapping our arms around both.

The fashion and makeup world is full of charts and creativity and color codes that promise to take any frumpy, somewhat overweight woman with dry, limp hair and turn her into a sparkling, olive, dynamic attractive *fox*. Research all the avenues. Try on all the styles until you put together a hairstyle, makeup combination, and clothes with a flair that make you proud of yourself.

We got a call one evening from some friends who had just been offered a beautiful condo. "The woman who owns it is very wealthy," my friend said, "and it's just seven steps from the ski slopes in upstate New York." Would we be interested in taking the children out of school for a couple of days and joining their family for a ski outing? I had to make arrangements for the baby, reschedule some clients (actually rearrange my whole life), but we did it. We drove through blinding snow, six hours (with me visualizing angels all around our car every time Tom sped past a semi splattering our car with snow). The next morning we all arose excitedly and began pulling on our layers of warm clothes as we watched the chair lift outside the window.

I remember fifteen years ago, when as a young elementary schoolteacher, my roommate talked me into ski lessons. I was teaching in Colorado at the time, where there is some of the best ski country anywhere in the U.S.A. I was twelve years old before I learned to ride a bike borrowed from a neighbor. I was the slowest runner and poorest hitter in every game of softball I had ever played. Growing up in Hawaii, I was required to take swimming lessons in fourth grade. I think it took me weeks before I would even consent to putting my nose under water. No amount of intimidation by my instructors (who pointed out how brave and courageous all the other children were) could move me into lowering my face an inch under the surface of the water. I had grown up feeling I was truly a motor moron. And here I had agreed to going *skiing?*

My roommates took me to buy proper ski clothing, an extravagant expense for a schoolteacher. By the time I got to the slopes for beginner lessons, I looked professional but was petrified of failure and even physical harm under my layers of new skiwear. I smiled at all the other properly laden skiers trying to present to them the image of a confident, experienced skier. I joined a group of mutually smiling dressed-up neophytes, and we headed for a baby slope. Our instructor taught us to snow plow, which consists of pushing on the inside of your skis until you make a big inverted V. I graduated from the class, still unable to do so without falling, but my two-hour lesson was up and my instructor pointed the way to the chair lift and hill he thought I could work on. Still trying to smile, I exhaustedly shuffled those huge, flat boards under my feet toward the lift.

For two years thereafter of skiing a couple of days each season, I think I succeeded in making a spectacular fall getting off the chair lift each time I went up. I actually began to develop serious anxiety as the lift neared the getting-off station, and I was prepared to make as harmless a fall as possible, hopefully not knocking down anyone else in the near-vicinity. One time I think I managed to plow into three people. Before we could even get up, we had to take off all our skis and untangle!

Following one of my dramatic falls, a young man, obviously an experienced skier, swished up beside me as I lay licking the snow off my face and commented, "Lady, I have skied for years and have never seen anyone fall as much as you. I'm going to follow you and see if I can help." At the bottom of the hill with his private, specialized help he convinced me I could tackle a bigger hill. Wanting earnestly to believe I wasn't as bad as it had appeared up to this point, I joined him on the chair lift and got off to face a narrow, steep hill meant only for advanced skiers, I'm sure. After three awful falls (in an attempt to save my life as I uncontrollably flew down the run), I emphatically refused to go another inch. They sent for the ski patrol who put me between his skis and snow-plowed me down the hill!

Now, fifteen years later, here I was with my husband and two of my three sons, eight years and five years, once again out to tackle chair lifts and numb toes and fingers and steep hills. But after many experiences of latching my ski boots and getting off chair lifts (I only fell once on this trip), and finally learning to traverse (zig-zag), I actually feel like I can say to someone who asks, "Do you ski?" "Oh, yes, I sure do." Now grant it, for those in chair lifts overhead watching me make my way down the hill, they are probably smiling at my overly cautious approach, but I know where I've come from! I can add to my circle of knowledge about myself that my body can do more than twenty years ago I ever dreamed it could do. And I'm convinced it can even do more than I realize today if only I will risk to take experiences. My eight-year-old son speeds past me with fearless confidence with his skis and what he can do. Even my five-year-old, after seven lessons, can confidently get off the chair lift and make it down a mile-long hill without falling or stopping. They have abilities far beyond mine, but that does not diminish my statement of success nor knock me out of the "club" of skiers. We can all get better from whatever point we are, and we can all feel proud of what it is we today have seen our bodies do.

I'm amazed that for the first fifteen years of my life I did absolutely nothing physical but vacuum the house every Saturday. I said to Tom one day, "I'm amazed I even grew up with so much missing in my development." I believe, however, that we all grow up with missing experiences we should have had. Perhaps the function of adult life is to put into our lives those things we find out are missing. To continue discovering what it is we haven't yet learned about our innate gifts and abilities. Humorously, we parents probably try to put into our children's lives what was missing in our own. Our children grow up asking us why we didn't give them other things and set out to see to it their children don't miss out on those great experiences.

For instance, I hate to cook. If my family is lucky, I create from scratch and recipes two meals a week. In between, we eat out or I pull frozen chicken and corn from the freezer and serve them with a cold drink. I live true to Benjamin Franklin's teaching that we are to "eat to live not live to eat." However, I can see my sons marrying real homemakers who have exotic aromas floating through the air as they step in the door after a long day's work!

Really, adult life is wonderful because we do have more control to reach out, explore, and expand ourselves. If our childhoods had been perfect and complete, adulthood would most likely represent boredom.

I challenge you to begin to do something with your body. Walk, run, jump rope, take swim classes or aerobics. Join the tennis class at the YWCA. Challenge your bones and muscles to see what new skill they can learn. For some of us, natural ability or early-life experiences leave us with great beginning handicaps, but there is always space for growth and experience and the excitement of taking a step, when for several months (sometimes years) all we knew how to do was crawl!

# ann

jan, i have never liked my body. you never seemed to notice our flaws as much as i did. to be as aware.

that night, when we were only six years old, & we ran into the living room to kiss mother good night. a woman from the church was visiting with her. we were barefoot. in our nightgowns. she told us she had never seen such crooked toes. i was humiliated. it never before dawned on me that toes were things of beauty. things to be noticed & commented on. for years & years after, i tried to never let anyone see my toes. they were a defect. the woman said so. when i was older, i noticed other people in sandals, barefoot. their toes were mostly crooked, too.

when we took swimming lessons (required) in hawaii, in fourth grade, i was so embarrassed. my skin was so white. everyone else's so brown. & i had a mole on my neck. it seemed horrible. the combination of both was so disturbing to me i couldn't even concentrate on the lessons. the instructor & all the other kids would surely notice. would obviously think me disgusting. reject me in their minds. it was torture every day we had to dress down. i think i could have been a good swimmer, but my feeling of ugliness around my body destroyed any confidence, any joy, even my concentration. just as when friends invited us to go to waikiki, swimming. if i could have splashed in the sand & water in a wet suit where no one would notice the white skin, the freckles on my shoulders. how they would perceive me spoiled it all. i watched the brown, clear-skinned bodies around me in envy.

do you remember when they made us, in high-school

gym class, don swim suits & stand in front of a long mirror while the others in the class watched? to study our posture, our figures? my tummy puffed out a little. the white skin. the feeling was horrible.

i never could hit a ball on softball days. on the ski slopes, even when i was older, i would collide with other skiers. one time, without telling anyone, i took the fast towrope to a high slope. wanting so to be good, & it looking so easy, i thought i would tackle it. then i got to the top, & the slope was *so* steep. straight down. i was paralyzed. quickly i collided with two other skiers & landed on the tip of one of their skis, breaking my tailbone. all because i so *wanted* to feel good about my body. that i could do something.

then there was my hair. teasing it. crying if it didn't seem just right. sleeping a certain way so as not to wreck it— never flopping on the couch, through high school, for fear my bouffant hairdo would get squashed. i so wanted to look pretty. people often commented about our clothes because mother made them, & they were usually lovely, but i cannot remember people ever raving that we looked pretty. the one thing i longed to hear more than anything else.

i remember going to a dermatologist. terrified. even being rejected by him was a crushing thought. i thought i was the only person in the world, besides you, with freckles on my shoulders.

"please, doctor, can you take these freckles off?"

"which ones? you have quite a few," he laughed. as if the whole idea was ridiculous. a waste of his time & skills.

"as many as you can."

he'd burn them off, & i would wear nighties with bare shoulders, & feel so wonderful & whole, & hope my family would notice how pretty it made me.

now, after years of more sun...more tanning...to look dark & beautiful (the two automatically have always gone together in my mind), i have new little freckles on my legs. even my tummy, from two-piece swimsuits & bad burns. i sit in the bathtub & count them, & pretend how pretty i'd be without them.

it seems people often comment about my fabulous figure, but the small rear & the flat tummy & the long-narrow legs seem insignificant because i see the little freckles instead. i don't even think anyone else notices. my husband doesn't. truthfully, the older i have become, & more observant, i see *lots* of people with a *lot* more freckles...and bigger ones...than i have. it doesn't seem to bother them at all. but it still does me.

once, i remember mother saying we all have compensations. some, good figures. some, beautiful skin. or teeth. or an instant charisma. i always notice people's skin. that's what matters most to me. someone else may always be observing weight.

jan, now i'm 39. you were there when i started running. you watched & cheered me through my first boston marathon. you & tom would drive along & clock me on 20-mile practice runs. even after running eight 26.2-mile marathons, & buying pretty clothes, & living in an environment where almost everyone is white, pale-skinned, i still get my saddest feelings around my body. around my physical limitations & appearance. i still cry once in a while, without will's knowing, because i feel in moments so ugly. aging skin. limp hair. & now, with pregnancy, my body shedding the trim, slim, waistline. bulging out. the fear now of even losing my figure. my one, truly positive physical asset.

the doctor took the mole off my neck years ago. my face has always been clear & rosy, if nothing else. my features are quite fine. nothing big or crooked or noticeable. will thinks i am beautiful, & even if i am not, it should matter a whole lot to me that he does.

yet i long to feel really good about my body. does one ever unlearn the feelings & attitudes around one's body from childhood?

at least i can talk about it today. for years, i would not dare. if people didn't notice, & i did not draw attention to it by talking about it, there would not be such great risk of rejection.

i have always feared rejection, more because i am not pretty enough or athletic enough, than for any other reason.

# 3.

# Assertiveness: Being True to Ourselves

## ann

somehow i must come up with a plan of asserting myself. of communicating my own ideas & feelings. of making my statements to the world in a creative way. helping you to know me not because my father is prestigious in the community, or my husband, or because some friend in a power position can get me all my interviews.

i had been out of college a few years, when i decided it would be fun to own a condominium & live in downtown boston. being a young dean of women on a small, liberal arts campus had certainly not brought wealth, but i had written two books by that time, which had made the inspirational best-seller lists, & that cushioned my small salary.

i had never balanced a checkbook, but was not a big spender, & so far had never overdrawn. however, if someone had tried to grade me on my financial/business expertise, i would have received a barely passing grade, i'm sure.

regardless, i crawled into my little sports car, & headed downtown from quincy, a suburb of boston. someone had mentioned a particular, old building on the waterfront that had been restored & was very elegant, exactly what charmed me.

walking in & asking for a certain realtor by name, i was directed to the fourth floor, & quickly found myself in a picturesque, stone-blasted brick condo, with high, old-beamed ceilings overlooking the boston harbor & dozens of yachts.

mind you, i knew zero about property value. about financial packages of any kind. of the concept of investment. it never crossed my mind that a real estate broker would tell my *anything* that was not absolutely honest & accurate. i was young.

i was on my own in the world. i had basically been very sheltered growing up in a struggling minister's home. but i had made a decision to live in boston, & i was trying, though ignorant, to find a good solution.

i looked. i listened. i believed every word the broker said about dozens liking the place, & one man who was to return in 30 minutes & put his $500 deposit down to buy. it was a studio apartment, but very glamorous & exotic & perfect, i thought, for a single woman like myself. an exorbitant selling price was quoted & i couldn't imagine where i could possibly get the monthly payments, but i so loved the place, & then & there wrote my own $500 check to purchase the condominium before this other man or one of the "dozens" would beat me to it.

an attorney was recommended by the broker for me to talk with who would handle all the legalities. at 25 years of age, i had never seen an attorney in any form of business, to say nothing of a hard-nosed, downtown-boston eastern one. ira feinberg came across, at first, rather hard & brash, but kind, & asked for my bank statement & tax statement of the previous year to see if i was even eligible.

"young lady, how do you expect to pay for this every month? i see you have money for a down payment, but your monthly income isn't very substantial!"

"well, mr. feinberg, i know you are not of my faith & probably will not understand, but i am a Christian, & i just feel that apartment is for me, & now that i am writing more, the money will be there."

he roared. "young lady, it's going to take more than Jesus & you every month."

"i understand that, sir, but i believe i can do it if you will give me the chance to try."

the bank took my money. there were a few moments, now & then, when i feared making the payments would be impossible, but every month the money was there. my next book & the next one came out, again best-sellers. i was invited, more & more, to speak across the u.s. there was the constant, simple salary from the college. mr. feinberg & his wife, andrea, became two of my best friends. favorite people.

ira shook his head at my wedding. i had married will

four years after, & had sold the condominium to move to idaho. that building in boston had become the most prestigious, prime place to live, & i more than doubled my profit, in cash, on the sale.

no one was there to help me make that decision to buy. to hold my hand. it was a risk. i was absolutely naive. but i knew if i was to progress with some of the desires in my heart, i must stand up, walk in, seek God's wisdom, try to be reasonable, yet not afraid to take a leap.

one of the most assertive things i did in junior high & high school was to try out for school plays. no one had ever told me i could act. basically, i was extremely shy & unsure of myself, but i wanted the recognition badly enough to swallow my fears, pick up the script, walk out on stage, & read some lines. they usually gave me very small parts, but that was better than nothing. it taught me poise. confidence. the fun of camaraderie with the cast. it gave me fresh courage to stand up & say, "i can."

i was invited once to address a large prison. stiff security everywhere. all the gates & doors were unlocked & locked as i was led to the large center where the prisoners were gathered. several hundred men, seated in rows of chairs. loud. rowdy. guards standing around, watching closely. i was plain & simple, with a Christian message of God & i in the world. the leader introduced me & i rose to address, not my first prison audience, but the most threatening. they laughed & coughed loudly & swayed in their chairs, incredulous that they had been brought in to listen to this young woman.

at moments, while i was speaking, i was fearful the place would erupt in riot. one could feel the rumblings right under the surface of the chaotic order. i never hesitated. my heart was beating hard, but i stood, squeezing the hand mike, & delivered my message with all the quietness & sincerity, but force, within me. it came to me that should they start booing, or walk out, i would remain until i was done with my 30-minute presentation because i believed in the message of love, & i refused to be intimidated. amazingly, they began to grow still & quiet. i began to notice tears glistening on faces here & there.

my message was not profound. it was the story of God & me & my struggles. i looked straight into their eyes. i did not waiver. my voice was steady. i was not there to impress, but simply to tell my story. eventually, the fact that they could not shake me up captured them, & caught their hearts off guard.

that is not the only threatening audience i had addressed. some university crowds have started off pretty rough. whistles & catcalls. but even the roughest, most callous heart is won by utter sincerity & quiet confidence.

after my address to a large convention, i was standing in the back by the table with all my books, autographing. several hundred people were gathered around me, visiting, when a young man pushed through the crowd, his face close to mine.

"i did not like your speech. you are a phony. half of what you said i do not believe."

my face began to flush & burn. everyone became very quiet & still. all focused on what i would say. how i would respond. it took me a few seconds to catch my breath. sucking in a mass of air, i quietly looked him in the eye & said, "i know sometimes i am not a real person, even though it is the one thing i desire as much as anything else. my speeches aren't too spectacular. you are right. but every word was from my heart, & i just hope you will pray for me. that is what i need the most. God can help me in a way no one else can."

he stared blankly, for an instant. was speechless. lost himself in the crowd. i resumed my signing of books & greeting warm, enthusiastic people. back in my hotel room later, i wept. exhausted. still overwhelmed by such a brash, harsh confrontation. but i did not let it shake or undo me. i was doing the best i knew. not even God requires more than that.

& there is a thread of truth in any criticism ever handed to us. i want to learn from it. to grow. to allow my critics to refine me, but not wash me out & beat me down.

wholeness is believing in yourself enough to stand & make a statement when it is needed.

when i married will, i so wanted to be a perfect wife. to have the happiest marriage. the most fulfilled man. i believed in submission. it is biblical. it did not make me feel inferior. only, that in the end, one person's judgment has to be chosen if the two are in conflict.

"ann, i want you to take these vitamins every day."

"jump in & go with me to the packing plant. i would like company."

well, i do take some vitamins, now, but...

"will, i refuse to take those three vitamins that are like rocks & taste so terrible. the others i promise to take faithfully. all my life i lived with one little multivitamin, & i have been healthy...& i am sure i will continue to be."

"honey, i normally would love to go with you while you check things out at the plant, but i am exhausted tonight. the baby has been fussy all day. the mail is stacking up at my office. i fly to new york tomorrow. this time, you will have to go without me."

always, i am trying to please will. he is very exciting to me, & i love him immensely. however, he is so strong & so forceful as a personality, that if i do not own something that is mine deep inside, & be true to me, i will lose the magic & sparkle i express to him. i will become hard & cold & distant. besides, a little independent spark & fire creates tremendous mystique & excitement to a marriage. a lot of surprise that generates the spirit of real romance. no one wants a *yes* person if one is healthy & wants to stretch.

i love the story of the little boy who wanted a puppy. he stopped at the pet store every afternoon, & petted & stroked the puppies. he called each by name. he saved his money.

one afternoon, he dug all the change out of his pocket & laid it on the counter, asking the pet-shop owner if it was enough for a puppy. he had been saving, & was ready to buy.

"you only have $1.57 & the puppies are $10."

the small boy walked quietly over to the pen, & started talking softly to the puppies. he was not overwhelmed. he would just keep working on his savings. the clerk was so touched by the child's spirit, he stepped over by him & said, "sonny, i think that money will do. pick whatever puppy you like, & it is yours."

he decidedly reached down & grabbed a certain puppy & nuzzled his face in the warm fur.

"honey, you do not want that puppy. he's crippled. he will never run with you in the park, or chase balls, or..."

"i know." pulling up his pant's leg, he revealed a steel brace to the man.

"i'm crippled, too. i will know how to be a good friend to this puppy."

& he limped out the pet-shop door, with the lame puppy under his arm, smiling.

we are all crippled, in different ways. sometimes, that crippledness makes us feel we have no real worth. we become intimidated & scared & overwhelmed. we hide behind someone else. we crumble when confronted. we believe whatever the world wants to tell us about ourselves, even if it is all negative.

wholeness says, i have weak, crippled places. sometimes you overpower me by your wealth or position or strong personality. but i have great worth. i am growing & learning. i feel deeply, too. & in my own way, moment by moment, i will teach you to value me. i will help you to see my worth. i will not be loud & pushy & obnoxious. but you will learn that i have beautiful, rich things to add to your life, even as already you are adding to mine.

# Jan

My father received a call to pastor a church in Portland, Oregon, when Ann and I were four years old. The people in that great church still report today that the first three months we were there neither Ann nor I would lift our eyes off the floor. We literally walked around with our heads hung down. We had come from the South with strong southern accents and were overwhelmed with all the attention we received.

Some of our parishioners in Hawaii, where my father pastored for ten years, ran into me about three years ago for the first time since I was eight or nine. They thought I was Ann. I was so outgoing. They claimed I seldom ever spoke as a child.

Ann was the firstborn and from that moment my leader. I think we grew up side by side with her as the "representative" of us both. When I was first married, I would love to go to a dinner party with Tom and Ann. I'd make certain they each sat on both sides of me, and for the remainder of the evening I could just sit in silence while they conversed with the guests.

For years I would crawl into bed at night and picture Christ standing in front of me. As intensely as I would try to bring my eyes to meet His and look at Him eye-to-eye, I honestly could not do it. I was not worthy enough. Even in fantasy I couldn't meet His eyes and have a sense of peace as a sinner who I felt had been redeemed. Maybe He *had* forgiven my sins, but I was still way too poor and needy to really connect.

Eye contact. Stopping and looking in your child's eyes,

your husband's, your boss's eyes, sends one of the most powerful messages you and I can make about ourselves. Looking into someone's eyes communicates, "I am a person over here. I feel I am worth receiving a response from you."

For too many years my whole sense of security was wrapped up in Ann. She'd fight my battles, solve my problems, and tell me what to do. I enjoyed for a season the temporary security that dependency brings. There were a lot of issues that for years I just never tackled. I'd call her and lay it at her feet, and she'd take care of it. What I didn't realize was that all those years she was taking care of things and taking risks and blazing the trails, which I would then follow, were giving her a sense of confidence and self-assurance and a much broader self-concept. But I was more unsure of myself than ever.

One of the most significant, life-changing decisions for us was our junior year of college, when we made the decision to go to different schools. Because of her involvement on campus, I was the one who was picked to go away. I was eighteen years old. My aunt and uncle lived near a small liberal-arts-college campus outside of Chicago, so it was decided that that is where I should go. I drove partway with my parents, and then in Kansas they put me on a train for Chicago.

I had never been one person in the world since conception in my mother's womb. Ann and I had not only spent nine months in a womb together but eighteen years in the same bedroom, same house, same school, and same church. I honestly didn't know who just "I" was. I probably knew better who Ann was. I had never walked out the door without her approval on what I was wearing and didn't know even how to roll my own hair.

My parents put me on the train through ankle-deep rain showers, handed me my suitcase, and I gasped, "Lord, it's just You and me now."

I was overcome when the students on campus liked just "me," and I began my search for who I was without Ann.

Inner confidence is born out of successful experiences. The first time I had to make arrangements to go home from Chicago, get to the airport, find the right ticket counter, change planes, and to my great amazement channeled my way home clear to Idaho was a confidence builder. Yahoo! I did it. I survived.

When Ann was out "changing the world," I was frantically looking for something significant to do, so I went back to graduate school. To be accepted in my graduate program I had to go before five professors and be interviewed. I had already started classes, and this was just a simple procedure. I was sure. Still, it was a terrifying step for me, to prove or disprove that I was in fact smart enough to receive a master's degree.

Two days after the interview I received a letter saying, "Mrs. Ream, we're not sure we know you well enough yet. Finish this semester's classes and interview with us a second time. We will then offer you a second chance."

I felt a sudden rush of nausea come over me. I had jumped out of my airplane ten thousand feet up and if my parachute didn't open I would splatter in shame below. But how would I ever know unless I had jumped?

I lived with a pulsating heart and sick stomach for the rest of that semester. How would I ever explain to the world that in fact I was *dumb*, a *reject*, if they did not accept me in the program?

There were days I'd come home from classes and say to Tom, "I know. Let's have a baby. Everyone would understand that. 'She couldn't finish her graduate work because she got pregnant.' "

I finished my course work and went through the interview the second time and was accepted. Every course I took and A I earned increased my confidence. I began to stand straighter and found it easier to look people in the eyes.

My sense of who I am has come through, taking leaps usually of great trembling in which I have explored new parts of me and found success. It is, as Ann said, a process. One successful experience stacked on top of another. Our confidence can not be wrapped up in someone else. We have no guarantees who is going to be with us tomorrow. My husband may die. My children will grow up. My sense of strength and inner confidence must come from my own awareness of what I have learned I can do and through my continuous building of positive experiences.

Many women test out "passive and dependent." They are in a pattern of letting others, often husbands, make decisions for them.

It is valid and mature to hear what others have to say and to ponder its truth for me and my life. But not anyone in the world outside of God knows better what I need than I do. Search deep inside yourself. Use words to convey to those around you what you need and desire. Respect your needs and represent them to others. People will treat us as good or poorly as we treat ourselves. If someone hurts your feelings, say, "Somehow, I feel hurt hearing you say that." If your friend wants you to enter some activity you don't feel comfortable with, say, "I don't want to hurt you but I don't feel comfortable with that. You go on, and I'll meet you later."

Learn to enjoy yourself. To sit at a cafe table, drink a cup of coffee, and smile at those who come in for breakfast. You are significant, even alone.

# 4.
# Why Did God Make Me?
## (Is There Any Purpose to Life?)
Jan

I was sitting with a young woman in therapy when she looked at me piercingly, wanting and needing an answer, and asked, "Why did God make me, anyway?" She caught me off guard, and I found myself repeating the question to regain some balance. It seemed I had surely answered that question for it sounded familiar. Yet as I repeated it, I was impressed by its depth and significance. I looked at her and honestly responded, "I'm not sure I've ever answered that question for myself. I'm not certain I know why God made me." She immediately, without a second's hesitation, looked at me and replied, "I know why God made you. He made you for me. I'd be dead today if it weren't for you."

As I reached out and took her hand, I reminded her that she needed me, but so did I need her. She was one of the reasons my life has meaning and purpose. "God made us for each other," I concluded.

William Glasser, the creator of Reality Therapy, claims that in order for a person to be healthy he must gain some worth and recognition. Basically, what he's saying is, *I must believe my life on this earth is worth something—has a purpose. If my life were to be wiped away—what would be missing on this earth?*

It's easier for me to tell you how God made you for me:

*Ann:* You have been my leader, someone to model my life after. You have led me to myself. You have challenged me to move way beyond my own natural instincts and drives. If you had not been born, I'm not sure I would have ever lived. I know

I never would have achieved. But I didn't want people to feel too sorry for me while you were soaring on to greatness, so I pushed myself further than I ever desired to grow. God put you on this earth to bring out my greatest potential.

*Tom:* You have helped me feel like I have value as a woman. You have accepted my body, and you think I am smart and enjoy listening to my thoughts. You, too, have encouraged me to expand my horizons and have applauded all my great moments. You've looked beyond my flaws and seen some beauty, and you have helped me to see it too.

*Cleora Handel:* My great friend and obstetrician who saw me through my last pregnancy and delivery, as a thirty-eight-year-old woman. You were with me every moment in the labor and delivery room. I felt special—a feeling I've yearned for all my life.

*Tre, Nash, and Christian:* You have given me mother-hood—the one thing I've aspired for all my life and you have helped me already see my weaknesses. In our lifetime together you will probably do more to reshape and refine me than any other humans on this earth. I used to believe God gave us children so we could train, teach, and lead them to adulthood and on to achieving great things. Now that I have three, I see God's cleverness so much clearer. He didn't give me children so I could have an opportunity to see my greatness, but rather so that I could see my weaknesses.

He also gave me you, Tre, Nash, and Christian, so that I could touch His incredible beauty and magic in you.

When you and I, Tre, lie on my bed and have deep, intimate talks about feelings and life, and I lie amazed by your deep wisdom for an eight-year-old...

And when you and I, Nash, run miles together, and I watch your indomitable spirit...

And Christian, when I roll you over and kiss you hundreds of times on your eyes and nose and fingers and toes and watch you communicate brilliantly your needs with no verbal language...

I know God made you to bring to me the greatest moments of life I will ever know.

In fact, this book is full of people who have opened up doors and windows of life to me—who for one moment or one season or all of my life have given me something I absolutely need or deeply desired and longed for.

For several years we lived in Shaker Heights, Ohio, where the houses are old, but quaint and full of charm. Our garage set several hundred feet behind our house, so we almost never parked in it. We would park in the driveway next to the front door. In the winter and nine months pregnant, I would cling to the railing and stumble to our car where, while the wind and snow destroyed my fresh hairdo, I would brush and scrape the snow and ice off my car. I dreamed of the luxury of an attached garage and a bathroom with a countertop around the sink and floors that didn't squeak when you walked on them.

Three years ago we were offered a beautiful four-bedroom, two-and-a-half-bath home in a luxurious area. It even had a laundry room connected to the kitchen! And best of all, it had an attached garage and the doors opened electrically. It was a gift from God. However, I first of all had to face the staggering reality of a move. I remember when I graduated from college. I ended up lying on my dorm-room bed crying, while my mother packed up my dresser drawers and belongings. I heard her mumble under her breath, "Where have I gone wrong as a mother?" For some reason, I develop paralysis when I get ready to move. It is absolutely overwhelming to me to face boxing up drawers and cupboards and bathroom shelves of half-used cologne and Estée Lauder cosmetic samples. After about an hour into this grueling job (with boxes and chaos everywhere), I develop a temporary emotional breakdown. I become completely weak and dazed and find myself scarcely able to function. I start discarding even the good stuff to keep from having to pack it!

A couple in our church with whom we were just acquaintances walked up to us the Sunday before we were to move on Friday and said, "We're going to come help you." I know God must have put it in their hearts to do so, because if they had known what they were getting into, I'm sure they would have planned a trip to the Caribbean to insure safety in distance.

Walter and Elaine arrived Friday morning and they began to orchestrate this process like highly trained professionals. Elaine would hand me a box and instruct me like a ten-year-old as to how to fill it. She did all the thinking—I just followed orders. She suggested instead of throwing piles into the trash that we would have a garage sale. Walter, a computer expert and executive, began to take tables and beds apart with incredible skill and speed. He and Tom began loading up their van and the U-Haul trailer.

By Friday night absolutely everything was loaded up and out of the house. It was almost fun. Saturday morning we headed for the new home and by Saturday night we hadn't just unloaded boxes and furniture in the middle of every room—literally every box had been emptied and every room was set up. Wayne and Kay, some other great friends, had come, and all the dishes and pots and pans had been put on the shelves. All I had to do was discover which drawer had what. It was like a miracle. Usually friends help for an hour or two and then claim legitimately some pending emergency at home (this is my approach, I know!) and leave you in seemingly as much chaos as when they arrived. Not Walter and Elaine. They weren't quitting until the job was done. It's no wonder they've been successful in life.

We crawled into bed that night, and it was like a fantasy. We even had our own bath in our huge master bedroom with a fireplace, cathedral ceiling, and balcony. I did not have to face getting up to one unpacked box. These people who had been only acquaintances became bonded friends for life. She also planned and organized a garage sale and we made three hundred dollars. I truly believe the greatest extension of their lives that year was seeing me through an ordeal that could have taken a tremendous toll on me psychologically and physically. Why did God make you, Walter and Elaine? Well, in the year 1982, in the month of July, God made you to see Tom and me through what could have led to near-divorce and a nervous breakdown if you hadn't given of yourselves. We will be debtors to you forever.

I truly believe God made each of you to be used by Him to touch and alter and inspire and detour me to where He needs me to be. There I can touch and help and be used to help others get to where they need to be. Then we can all find more of Him and prepare for eternity.

I honestly feel that what I have to give you is so insignificant and trite. There's my honesty. The touch of my hand to yours. My listening heart that is not judgmental. My deep belief in your uniqueness and power as an individual. My openness to hear what you have to say. But I extend them all to you. If in some quiet moment I can touch your life and make a difference, then my living will not be in vain. And please keep giving away what you have. No one can replace you or give what you alone can give. We can stand in this world for each other.

I think it's important to remember God did not make me to touch everyone. There are some of you who don't need or want what I have to give. It does not make you bad or me ineffective.

It is only vital for me to keep giving away what I have—when and where it is needed. And when there is something I need or desire I am going to ask God to bring you into my life. It is as we give to each other that we both find worth and meaning to life.

In 1977, Ruby and Lloyd took my first baby, Tre, into their arms and lives to care for him during the hours I had therapy sessions. They hugged him, sang to him, and let him kick in the sunshine with not even a diaper on. They poured all the love they had into my wonderful little son and gave him a great sense of worth and value.

Today I have Cathy and Nancy to wrap up my three children into their arms and homes and help them feel they really do belong somewhere while I am away, listening and wrapping my arms around others in my office. No one could ever convince me otherwise—that for these moments God made these wonderful, loving, giving people for Tom and me and our children—to give of their great resource of love so I can give what I have.

When I called Jan McClennan to thank her for all the

beautiful clothes she helped me find and buy (see Chapter 8), she responded, "You are the one who taught me how to love. If I have added to your life some joy, I'm thrilled." That's why God made you—that's why God made me.

# ann

when i was a small girl, i felt i was somehow a special person. destined to make some unique impact on the world. chosen by God to someday do great things. as i have become an adult, over & over again i have heard people tell me the same thing. that they, too, felt special, with unique destinies. maybe we all need to feel that in some deep, inner place so we can throw ourselves into the challenge of living.

i remember one afternoon when i was about eleven. my mother brought an alcoholic woman home for the afternoon & dinner. she was drunk, & crying, & it was my job to walk with her next door to the church my father pastored, & play a lot of old hymns to her. as i played the hymns, & she cried, i felt God made me to help her feel loved.

for years, i felt God made me to help jan move beyond her insecurities & fears & make a mark on the world. i was always trying to coax her into things. to writing a poem. to entering a speech contest. to running for some student government office. I felt i was her protector. i coaxed her through long bike rides & evening runs when we were older. i shared all my clothes with her. i took care of her...until she passed me by, & started taking care of me.

for years, i wakened with one prayer,

> God, make me creative today.
> help me love people for You.

& in every day, i would search for opportunities to

46

touch people's lives. ice-cream cones for ghetto children. holding them in my lap. little songs for cab drivers in rush-hour traffic on hot, crowded afternoons. a $20 bill slipped to someone struggling. a cup of hot chocolate for the maintenance man when i heard the vacuum cleaner in the hall outside my apartment. taking an inner-city child from the asphalt jungle on a trip so he or she could see the beauty & wonder of the world outside.

for five years, i was a college dean of women. when i started i was scared. afraid i was incapable of the position. more & more i began to feel i was to be authoritative & no-nonsense, but loving & fair. sometimes i failed. got unjustifiably angry, & yelled. had to call a girl back in & apologize. sometimes i gave a girl one chance too many, & she took advantage of me. but i always felt God made me to touch & encourage & bless people's lives. to make their loads easier. to give youth vision & the courage to dream dreams. to inspire college kids to overcome anything, with God's help, & in simple, kind ways help me change the world.

never did i have ambition to write books & speak to thousands. i wanted only to marry & be a mother. when a publisher asked me to write about some of my experiences, i did …feeling very self-conscious & shy. when my first little book became a best-seller, i decided God must have made me to be a simple woman who reminded people to love. to reach out. to take God's word & believe for anything. this is my tenth book, & for years, i have tried to do that.

God made me to be creative for Him. i know that. i just did not know how hard it would be, at times, for Him to keep me humble enough & sensitive enough. to teach me about life so i could adequately relate & comfort those around me who were trying to live.

God made me with special ideas in mind, but i wish i could have been in on the planning. my skin would have been more olive-colored, & flawless. my hair more coarse, with some curl in it. my shoulders broader. my eyes wider-spaced. i would have completely removed the lazy part in me that i have to fight with all the time.

God must have made me to fail, too. i sure have done a

lot of that. in spite of all my efforts, & knowing God loves & forgives me, i still carry a great deal of pain around regrets. things i would like to undo. moments i wish to obliterate.

one that haunts me happened about ten years ago. a very distinguished, powerful man in the government heard me speak at a big army base. his life was seemingly, deeply touched. he wrote me several times, & suggested he come to boston some evening from washington, d.c., for dinner. he was divorced. i knew that. very attractive. brilliant. somehow i never connected to the fact that he was really hungry for truth. i classified him with most men. someone pursuing me as a woman.

wanting to touch his life, but insecure & wanting him to like me as a woman, i put on a sort of revealing cotton dress. not anything embarrassing or bad, just something that suggested more than the "simple, young woman with a dream" that he had heard me speak about.

i remember that evening. rather than being totally true to who i was & what i stood for...the reason that brought him to boston, that drew him in his search for something deeper...i tried to relate to him as an appealing woman. talking on a more superficial level. trying too hard to be effusive. he flew back to washington, d.c., & i began to be racked with the pain of failure. of knowing God had put this man in my life for me to be real & simple & honest with. instead, i had worried about my significance as a woman. always, i will believe i lost a tremendous opportunity to help a searching man find God. to this day, i pray that in some crowded airport or on some street corner, i will run into him...and be able to apologize.

God has made me to fail so i will know what it truly means to be human, & lost, & to need Him. so that my compassion will be deep & my sensitivity keen. so my love will be purer & more redemptive in a hollow, superficial world.

God made me so that now, when my parents are aged & forgetful & not so strong, i am here to look after them. to make them laugh. to tell them they are not alone. to help them not fear old age. to bring grandchildren in the front door. to remind them they are still useful, still significant.

in the deepest places in me, i believe God made me for will anderson & he for me. to cover the areas where he is not as strong. to encourage him when the business deal falls through, or the potato season is bad. to curl up beside him at night & listen to his secrets. to the deepest, most real feelings in his heart. to ride bikes with him. to go fishing. He made me weak in areas so will's strength could pull me along, so there can be camaraderie in our union.

God made me for taylor & brock, my little sons. & for hilary & natalie & erika, the neighborhood girls, when they knock on the front door & need a friend.

He made me for you, right now, to tell you that you matter. you count. there are tears, but there are sunrises, too. to remind you to believe in something bigger than yourself, & to not give up. not ever.

God made me to be happy in His plan. to not wish i were someone else. to not let mountains level me. to not always be looking back with nostalgia. to walk with my face toward the sun. toward the promise of tomorrow.

most of the time, in spite of the success God has allowed to come my way, in spite of many people that love me & are kind, i confess i have a hard time remembering God made me for all this. that i absolutely have worth. that i am important in His scheme of things.

for most of life, i think we fight God. we keep trying to show Him what we were made for. we keep giving Him better ideas. we keep working for something bigger & greater than anything He seems to have in mind. for many of us, by the time we are in midlife, we feel we somehow have missed out on some of the great things we were born for. we fight with God over this.

i come to you, knowing God made me not to impress you. not to be on book covers. not to be an authority. not to be perfect or a genius. not to make a million dollars!

God made me to be uncomplicated in my faith. to watch children & kites & sunsets & rainbows & enjoy them. to take your hand regardless of who you are or how you look. to listen to you. to accept you right where you are. to love you unconditionally.

God made me to be real. to be honest. to be open. to never compare myself to you, but to strive to become my own best person. to have character & dignity.

God made me to be ann
i am trying to like me more & more.
to be happy in His plan.
in this, i can know wholeness.

# 5.
# *Vulnerability*
## Jan

I remember going to a concert one evening with my parents when I was eighteen. At that point in my life I was a body, well-dressed, my hair smooth and flowing, my cheeks pink from some sun. I looked normal. I smiled, shook hands, and could converse socially. A man came up to speak to my parents, looked at me, and commented about my attractiveness and how grown-up I had become. A smile creased my face, I thanked him, and he would never have guessed the thoughts hidden under my smooth exterior. *You're wrong. I'm really dumb, inferior. I can only look good for a moment. But if you stay with me longer than a moment, you too will see what a disappointment I am.*

I was eighteen, and no one had ever modeled for me what it meant to put into words what one is really thinking and feeling inside, and tenderly hand them over to someone who will take them and turn them into beauty. In all my eighteen years I can't remember ever hearing someone confess to feelings of inadequacy or humiliation or stupidity. It was clear I was the only human so stupid and inept, and I must make sure no one ever found me out!

When I was twenty-seven, engaged to be married, the women of the church I attended gave me an elegant bridal shower. It was in a huge, gorgeously decorated gymnasium. They were sure hundreds would come and had rows of brightly papered tables for people to put their gifts. By the end of the evening, only a few of the tables had gifts, and I had spent the evening smiling till my face felt permanently cemented into a smile, trying to conceal the stabbing humiliation to the hostesses that I obviously wasn't as loved as they had perceived. The next day I was in bed sick—sick with pangs of disappointment and hurt. As the phone rang in my apartment asking about the shower, I gave a glowing report but felt desperately in need of finding out if what I perceived had happened was reality. Yet I had never heard anyone confess to such "littleness," such disgusting feelings of inferiority. I must not expose how sinful and bad a person I was.

When I went back to graduate school at twenty-eight and heard people for the first time reveal feelings of jealousy, failure, shyness, insignificance, I felt an ecstatic relief. What do you know! I wasn't the only defective human, and I began to find freedom as I would risk to expose my deeper self. Only as we confess our inner feelings can we shed light on how valid or realistic they are.

I knew a man who was rigid and judgmental and bigoted. One night I looked him squarely in the eyes and said, "I don't know why you are so harsh and critical toward struggling humanity. I only know if I fell from grace, if I really ever blew it, you are the last person on earth I'd ever confess my failures to."

One of the most vulnerable, open people I've ever met is my friend Kay. She has taught me more about openness than any professor I had in graduate school. Early in our relationship she would cautiously hand me her real self, her raw wounds, her feelings of inadequacy, and I found the courage to share more of mine.

I've heard my husband who is not a therapist say, "You choose someone who you've tested out as kind and then start handing them a little bit of string at a time. If they receive your string with honor and acceptance, then you can give them more. If not, find someone who will."

One of the biggest reasons people line up outside of therapists' doors is that there is this great need to shed our masks and discover if we still are worthwhile and valuable and even so-called normal. To be truly known and still valued.

I cannot accept the seeming unpleasant, negative parts of myself until I find someone else who can, and then I am free to grow beyond them.

I had seen this young woman I'll call Sally for a year and a half professionally before she finally confessed to having an affair with her boss. Many times she would come to her session and say almost nothing. Always staring at the floor. There were days she would abruptly look at me and say, "I want to leave now." Following her confession of her affair and my meeting her with love, she poured out more of her troubled past and her hidden secrets—her incestuous relationship with her father and a sexual encounter with another woman. While she was taking enormous giant risks to reveal her unacceptable behavior, she was very reserved. I wondered if this woman would ever really trust someone with her heart again.

One session she handed me a note. It read:

Two weeks ago you took my hand and squeezed it, and for the first time in eight years since I was so badly rejected I let myself feel some love. After I left I was full of this screaming inside me, this screaming to have you hold my hand again and let me try to squeeze back and look into your eyes. I think I'm ready to live again.

I put the paper down. She sat rigid across from me twisting a hanky in her hand and staring at her lap. For a second I felt a sense of risk too. What if she didn't respond? I picked up her hand and held it in both of mine. Her hand was limp and lifeless. We sat in silence for what seemed like hours. I finally said, "Sally. Can you feel me squeezing your hand?" She nodded. "Sally. Can you squeeze mine back?" Slowly I began to feel the pressure of her grasp. Her face became contorted as she squeezed harder and the tears began splattering down her face and mine, as she took the leap to love again—to knock down the last brick in her wall so she could touch the world again— *and be touched.* We hugged and she looked me purely in my eyes, and there was peace and freedom shining all over her face.

There are nights I reach over and softly but firmly rustle Tom into consciousness and, weeping, ask if he will talk to me. He doesn't push me away and tell me to wait till morning. He props up the pillows and in the stillness of the night hears me talk of my humanity and loves me. He helps me find my way out of the jungle by just accepting my words.

I can call Ann and pour out my ugliest, most embarrassing feelings and behaviors, and she cries and identifies and helps me believe I can rise to something better.

I have friends like Phyllis, who is willing to share some

of her feelings of grief around her motherhood, and I am comforted that not every mother out there feels like a supermom with flawless children.

I thank you Kay and Ann and Phyllis and Tom and all those in my life who have shared with me deeper pieces of themselves and have let me expose more of me. As much as any human skill I've learned, it has brought me closer toward friendship with myself.

## ann

my last book *Taste of Tears…Touch of God* was about my infertility. the wrenching, defective, screaming, yelling pain of not getting my body to do the right thing. (as if God had nothing to do with the miracle of conception.) it is a story of being stripped. all the layers peeled off, one by one, from all the years of growing up. the layers that covered my true self. that tried to hide my fears & inferiority & uncertainty. that worked at showing the world, & myself, how strong & invincible & brave & courageous i was.

i bled in that book. i confessed things… feelings…never before revealed. i displayed my ugly parts. the tiny seed of nothingness i felt about me.

yesterday, in a letter from a woman who has read all my books, she told me *Taste of Tears…*was a disappointment. there was so much pain in it. so much weakness. all my other books were so radiant & positive & inspiring.

barbara walters, in one of her specials, interviewed burt reynolds. years ago, but i'll always remember. "if you someday have a grandchild, & set him on your lap, what will you tell him?"

"that i'm never enough for the world. they always want more."

in so many situations in my life, that has been true. no matter how real i have tried to be (and granted, i am a lot more real today than i was in book 3 or 4…process has led me there). no matter how much vision & wonder & joy i have worked to put into life…nor how vulnerable…it never seems enough.

it is very scary to be vulnerable. the world always wants something more spectacular & exciting than one's flaws & fears & struggles. but unless i am vulnerable, i can *never* be whole.

father john powell says, "i am afraid to tell you who i am. if you do not like it, it is all i have."

one day, at my grandmother's, when i was four or five, i ran by a small coffee table & accidentally brushed a little glass dish onto the floor, shattering it. i quickly scooped up all the broken pieces & hid them under the piano. then my grandmother would not know what happened, or who did it.

she quickly discovered the dish missing. pulling jan & me aside, she asked, "who broke the dish?"

"i didn't," jan said, with innocent, wide-eyed sincerity.

"i didn't," i replied.

"well, one of you did, & God knows. He never forgets. when you die, He adds all these things up. so you better tell me the truth," spoke my little grandmother sternly.

somehow, i had not thought of her bringing God into it. to have Him know this lie i told, & confront me with it years & years down the road was more painful than i could imagine.

"grandma, i did it. the pieces are under the piano."

it was the first time i can remember the vivid pain, & freedom, of being vulnerable enough to say i failed. i was wrong. i was bad.

for years after with my already built-in fear of rejection, i did not tell anyone bad things about myself. jan was always more honest. she would readily admit to getting a *D* in astronomy or not doing well in sports. i would wince.

"jan, i do not EVER tell people those things. they will wonder about you. only tell them good stuff."

always, i worked at dropping little comments about the A i received. i always said boys did not interest me because it seemed awful that anyone would notice no boy ever seemed to go for me. never NEVER would i admit to anyone, growing up, that i did not like my body. people might *really* notice it, & feel more negatively than ever.

when jan & i, in high school, put our names on the ballot & ran for songleader for the football games, it was the most vulnerable experience to that point. we did not discuss it with anyone. i always slipped into the after-school rehearsals, hoping not even the fellow competitors would notice & think us crazy to believe *ANYONE* would vote for us.

as they announced the winners' names over the loud-speaker system, we were stoic. never had i felt such rejection & defeat, & the taste ripped through my body & left me weak & sick. but not one word about it was spoken. when we arrived home, we walked quietly, soberly to our bedroom, past my mother who asked, "how was your day?"

"fine."

i experienced the second most vulnerable experience of my life. throwing myself across my bed, beside jan's, we both buried our faces in our pillows & stifled wrenching sobs.

though jan was my closest person in the world… though we had shared the womb together…though she knew more about me, & i, her, than anyone, it was our first truly open acknowledgment of embarrassment & pain. i even was afraid to be that open with her.

once, when i was young & visiting my aunt & uncle with jan, i found scissors & cut all my eyelashes as short as i could. my aunt asked me if i had done something to them, & i said, earnestly, "oh, no." only years later, as a high schooler, did i have the courage to confess my lie. it seems so silly now, but at the time, it was brave.

one can't be totally vulnerable all at once, i do not think. it happens gradually. it comes as one is willing to risk. to be absolutely honest with oneself. to cautiously reach out & be open with someone else. one brave confession builds on an-other.

there was the time i confessed to my friend rhonda that i was threatened by her. jealous of her beauty. & the mo-ment i walked forward in a large church, to kneel at the altar, alone, & confess to God i needed Him. that i had sinned. with rows of people, well dressed & so proper, seated behind me.

some people feel that sharing a feeling about oneself is vulnerable. to me, only when i tell you something about me that is risky to how you will feel…that reveals how weak i am…how human…how far from noble. only then does a miraculous & wonderful change occur in our relationship & in my level of wholeness. in my ability to build my worth not in my strengths but in my ability to take both strengths & weaknesses & use them in becoming *real*.

a very dear friend…one of the men i most respect …an assistant football coach…borrowed something from someone else's desk. no one was around & it seemed logical to him to just use it & return it later.

shortly thereafter, in a session with players & coaches, the head coach made a big deal about this particular piece of equipment missing. he was abrupt & upset, & asked if anyone knew anything about it. my friend was terribly embarrassed, & had not realized he had done anything serious. he remained silent, saying nothing. a few days later, in another large meeting, he stood to his feet. a grown man. a tremendous reputation. respected. with sincerity, he confessed his error. his fear in being embarrassed. he talked about his lack of honesty & his conscience.

that was vulnerable. risky. digging down into some deep, inner reserve. being willing to confess he was not all hero. he was frail sometimes. he failed. who could love him less? it takes so much more courage to reveal one's fears & failings than one's joys & strengths.

i have lied in my lifetime. i have accused others of something i myself was afraid of. felt inferior more times than i can count. been jealous. had impure thoughts. everyone should hold on to some mystery, but i am tired of all of us sitting side by side in churches & offices & schools, looking so smug, so together, so happy. & underneath we are alcoholics or crooks or angry & deceiving. sometimes dying. & scared. fragile.

PLEASE HEAR WHAT I'M NOT SAYING
author unknown

Don't be fooled by me.
Don't be fooled by the face I wear.
For I wear a mask. I wear a thousand masks.
Masks that I'm afraid to take off.
And none of them are me.

Pretending is an art that's second nature with me;
But don't be fooled, for God's sake don't be fooled!
I give you the impression that I'm secure.
That all is sunny and unruffled in me.
Within as well as without.
That confidence is my name and coolness my game.
That the water's calm and I'm in command.
And that I need no one.
But don't believe me.

My surface may seem smooth, but my surface is my mask.
My ever-varying and ever-concealing mask.
Beneath lies no smugness, no complacence.
Beneath dwells the real me, in confusion, in fear, in aloneness.
But this I hide.
I panic at the thought of my weakness and fear of being exposed.
That's why I frantically create a mask to hide behind.
A nonchalant, sophisticated facade to help me pretend.
To shield me from the glance that knows.
But such a glance is precisely my salvation!

That is, if it's followed by acceptance.
If it's followed by love.
It's the only thing that can liberate me from myself.
From my own self-built prison walls.
From the barriers that I so painstakingly erect.
It's the only thing that will assure me of what I can't assure myself...
That I'm really worth something...
But I don't tell you this, I don't dare...I'm afraid to.
I'm afraid your glance will not be followed by acceptance and love.
And your laugh will kill me.

I'm afraid that deep down I'm nothing, that I'm just no good.
And that you will see this and reject me.
So, I play my game, my desperate pretending game.
And my life becomes a front.

I dislike the superficial game I'm playing.
The superficial, phony game.
I'd really like to be genuine and spontaneous, and me,
But you've got to hold out your hand...
Even when that's the last thing I seem to want or need.
Only you can wipe away from my eyes the blank stare of the breathing

Dead...
Only you can call me into aliveness...

Each time you are kind and gentle and encouraging.
Each time you try to understand because you really care.
My heart begins to grow wings...
Very small wings, very feeble wings, but wings.
With your sensitivity and sympathy, and your power of understanding,
You can breathe life into me.
I want you to know that.
I want you to know how important you are to me.
How you can be a creator of the person that is me, if you choose to...

It will not be easy for you.
A long conviction of worthlessness builds strong walls.
The nearer you approach me, the blinder I may strike back;
It's the irrational, but despite what the books say about man,
I'm irrational!!

I fight against the very thing that I cry out for.
But I am told that love is stronger than strong walls, and in this
Lies my hope.
My only hope.
Please try to beat down these walls with firm hands.
But with gentle hands, for a child is very sensitive.
Who am I, you may wonder?
I'm someone you know very well.
For I am every man or woman you meet.

# 6.
# *Sexuality*

## ann

i must talk about my sexuality because it was a very big issue in my life. it was not something i was able to resolve overnight, but again, a process that led me out of a lost place into the light.

always, for me, sexuality was limited to intimacy, & even as a little girl, i craved feeling close to people. there never seemed to be enough of that for me. my mother was always very warm & physical as i can remember & my father...but after questioning my mother, she said she would put jan & me in our big bedroom, with all our toys, & close us in with a gate. she would cook, clean house, get things done, & leave us to play for hours. we were twins. she did have a five-year-old son too. it may have nothing to do with it, but nonetheless, i have craved more intimacy all my life.

nakedness...no secrets...no inhibition seemed to always make me feel secure.

when my father would pull my mother down into his lap in her exquisite negligee, & hold her & kiss her, i loved it. it seemed so free. so open. so warm.

there was a family who had three small children, & they would bring their pajamas & let them change in the car on late nights, before they got home. once in a while, jan & i would be invited to spend the night, & it was such an experience for me to get undressed in the dark, with all the others, & put my pajamas on. it made me feel so close & whole.

as i went through college, & the first couple of years out, i was very naive. being raised in a strict religious home, i grew up believing my virginity was more sacred & valued than

ANYTHING, & to lose it would be so serious & devastating that i would never recover. my life would be in crisis.

teaching school in kansas city was my first job out of college, & i shared an apartment with a beautiful girl, several years older, getting her master's degree. she began to tell me about this dashing, fortyish man who lived across the hall. she could see him come in, & watch him through the peephole on our door. there was a "dr." before his name on the mailbox, which made us think him even more exciting & dashing (we learned later he was a veterinarian).

one saturday afternoon, while my roommate was at the library, this gentleman knocked on our door, & with an engaging smile, said he hoped i would be home. could i join him for dinner at his apartment that evening? flushed & overwhelmed, i stammered out a yes, & closed the door. barbara was much more intrigued by him. i had only started noticing because of her raves, & though i felt complimented at the invitation, it was obvious she would have handled him much better than i. i was twenty-one & naive to the extreme.

he was very slick...suave. (lovely, intimate dinner with candlelight.) almost before i knew what was happening, he had me on the thick rug, kissing & caressing me. the conflict of feelings in me, all those years until 21, it never occurred to me that men would really find me exciting. though i had dated a lot in college, i was quite distant...very removed...& remained very casual.

so there i was, on the floor with this savvy, mature man. excited. trembling. complimented, but scared. i quickly struggled out from under him, & stumbled to the door, muttering "thanks" & "good night" & fell through my door across the hall, shaken. though nothing specific had happened, i felt ravaged by guilt & fear that clung to me for weeks. cautiously, i came & went from the apartment, trying to avoid that man.

maybe i am wrong, but it seems to me that many men are attracted to women who are bright, on-the-outside self-assured, confident, & successful. the more i succeeded with my books, the sharper my clothes looked, the more attractive i became to men.

suddenly, i went from a rather plain, conservative, rigid, prim girl to a more flamboyant, confident, warm, & effusive woman. i was shocked that men reached out to me. wanted to take me to lunch & dinner. flattered me constantly. picked my brain. treated me with such respect & value. sought my body.

& i began an enormous struggle within myself to try & resolve my sexuality as a woman. as a God-fearing woman all my life i had felt physically ugly & unappealing. for years, i had longed for affirmation as a person. reassurance. always feeling this craving to be close to people, yet guarded, & removed.

i got lost. for a while i was allured by the attention. it was confusing to me. was it how i looked in a bikini or letting a man get close to me that made me a real woman? that brought me intimacy?

the worst part was that even married men were always making overtures. men i respected. men who had charming, fabulous wives. men who claimed strong Christian standards. it blew me away into a vacuum of despair & fear. how would i ever be able to trust a man?

one day, walking along a beach in florida, warm sun & breeze in my hair...cold, salt water lapping over my toes...a deep, shaking truth swept over me. as it began to take hold of some deep, inner place in me, i felt cleansed & purified. i began to see truth, & truth immediately started setting me free.

sexuality is not wrapped up in what i do or do not do with a man. my value as a woman...my femininity...my appeal...my sensual beauty...comes from deep inside me. a warmth, a charm, a spirit that is quietly confident in saying, "i am a woman. i love that. i will share my heart & soul with you, but for me, only when i marry & make a lifelong commitment to a man will i express the totality of that in a complete physical sense. oh...i might like to throw my arms around you. or have you hold me. or dine with candlelight. or stroke your arm. but you can not make me feel pressured & pulled to prove my sexual gifts to you...my feminine charm...by some physical act."

it began to create in me a strength & self-respect i did not know i had. there was more harmony in me. more peace. i no longer felt pressured by desire & tempting words, &

afterwards, sorry, for whatever i had been willing to give.

more & more, i nurtured my great need for intimacy by relating more to couples. to children. to sharing my feelings with a man, & then quietly saying "good night" & going home with a sense of such fulfillment within myself. around a loving God. of strength in knowing who i was without having to prove it to satisfy a selfish desire.

the more i built my world around others, & activities, & serving & touching the wounded & broken, the less my sexual desires overwhelmed me. the less confused i was about my own value & worth, & the need to prove it before i was accepted.

i gave my life away, not to the allures of men who were always asking me to prove something to them...but to anyone on a feeling, caring level. never before had i so felt i had captured femininity & true sexual appeal. never before had i lived with such serenity & self-worth.

now i'm married.

will never compromised before he married. his idealistic visions of sex only fit into a marriage context. he was a very hard worker. highly motivated. tremendous athlete. all his energies were locked into achieving in those areas.

he was 38, & i was 35. being a scholar...a collector of data...he had read every book he could find on sex. he was relaxed & free & creative & masculine.

as a wife, i am ready to be my husband's lover in the bedroom. it matters to me that i meet will's needs, & he is not tempted to look elsewhere. however, because sexuality, to me, always equates intimacy, i still sometimes struggle.

will, on the other hand, is a no-nonsense man. for him, there's no excuse for not getting any job done. he is an idea man. goal-oriented. academic in his thinking. he is not interested in real human interest drama on t.v., he watches science fiction or an old western or a tennis match.

we have had to work intensely on building more intimacy into our marriage. his sharing deep feelings with me. i, with him. his being willing to hold me or lie close to me without always wanting sex. just to comfort & reassure me & visit with me.

before i married, it was easy to feel seductive by the way a man & i looked at each other. or a touch. today, married, the most seductive thing will can do to me is to care for the children while i clean up the kitchen or take a quiet, hot bath. it is helping me around the house, or taking care of some little thing that i have asked him to check.

even the way he looks affects me. sometimes his hair is so disheveled. he has the same shirt on for the third day. no matter if he is rugged & strong & very masculine in physique...and if his flashing, black eyes captured me...if he looks too sloppy, i am turned off.

more than ever, i know sexuality is not wrapped up in our bodies...in an act. it is a spirit. an internal aura. it is not will's body that turns me on; not his techniques. it is who he is as a man. how he views life. how he lives it out. how he treats others. how secure & strong he is within himself. how he manages our home. his integrity. his fairness. those issues make him the exciting, sexual person he is to me.

he would say the same about me, i think. oh, he loves my body. it is appealing to him, but it is my ability to think & share ideas with him. the avoidance of nagging. the mothering of the babies. my spirit of serenity. my ability to be happy. to enjoy life. to share in things he likes to do. to laugh easily. to have faith & trust in him. to not fret & worry all the time.

one of the most sexually exciting things i have ever done with will is to cross-country ski. his big, strong body in knickers & heavy sweaters & goggles pushing his skis recklessly, quickly across frozen lakes & through trees & down hills. confident. full of energy. ecstatic with the elements of outdoors. that turns me on & fulfills me more than any foreplay or candlelit bedroom. it is something we truly share. it is not smothering. it is not possessive. not demanding.

i love being a woman.
lotion & perfume & lingerie &
warm rugs in front of a blazing fire.
carrying a baby on my hip or in my womb.
surprising will with a lemon-meringue pie.
sticking a note on his pillow when i must fly somewhere to speak.

i love having something that is mine separate from will & the babies. my writing. my lecturing.

i love exercise. a fast walk. a ten-mile run. some tennis.

i love going to church & sitting beside anyone...another human spirit...struggling as i am. singing together. praying. hearing a child stand & share a hurt. ask for help.

it's all of this that makes me truly a woman. that expresses my sexuality. my womanhood. my feminine spirit.

frankly, i believe all of this in the heart & soul of a woman can do more if properly expressed, to shape & change the world for good, than anything else.

# Jan

It was 11:00 P.M. and Tom and I had just crawled into bed. Tom rolled my way, wrapped his arms around me and the stage was set for what was to come. I lifted my head just enough to see the clock, and when I realized how late it was I groaned, "Oh, honey, we've got to hurry with this. It's eleven o'clock, and I have to get up at six."

A year before when I had married Tom Ream I had said to him, "Women keep pulling me aside and reminding me sex is just a very small part of marriage. Most of your life is wrapped up in grocery shopping, cleaning, house, work, and so forth, they would say. Honey, I don't want to be like all these other women. I'm twenty-seven years old and I've waited all my life for this. Please promise me we can have sex all the time, if we want it."

There are many nights, however, when I crawl under the sheets and passion is the furthest thing from my mind and the closest to his. And I know Tom, in disbelief, must remark to himself, *This is not the woman I thought I had married.*

Many women who come to me for therapy express the same kinds of feelings about their sexual relationships with their husbands. In fact, their concerns occur in three areas:

1. *Sexual satisfaction in marriage can be hard to achieve.*
We marry expecting glorious and wondrous explosions in the bedroom. I could write a book about all I've heard that has happened on honeymoons but not what was expected!

Achieving orgasm can be a difficult thing for many

67

women. It sometimes takes months and even years to develop a sexual relationship in marriage that brings the desired outcome, especially for the wife.

There are different levels of orgasm, and even if what you are experiencing in bed is good, we seem to ask ourselves, "But is it as good as what I just read about in my latest novel or *Ladies Home Journal?*" Women seem to be extremely concerned as to whether they are really having it, and men are trying desperately to get us to have "it," and often couples live feeling disappointed and uncertain about their sexual life.

It seems that orgasm has become the goal of a sexual relationship in marriage, rather than two people coming together and developing an art of sharing their total selves with each other, or of knowing the lovely joy that comes from experiencing the body, spirit, and mind of the man we have joined for life.

*2. The second major complaint in therapy is that after marriage sexual drive for most women diminishes.*

I've had many husbands tell me, "I think my wife could go the rest of our married life and not care whether we made love again. Now before I married her, mind you, I could hardly handle her passion."

You see so much of making love is a brain thing, an emotional response, not a physical one for a woman.

I'm somewhat amused as I stand back and look at it. When I was single, I was driven to affirm my worth as a woman. In this society marriage announces I've passed the "worthwhile female" test. I've been chosen. Singleness in our society carries with it a DEFECTIVENESS stamp. If I am really a valuable, worthwhile woman, I will be sought after, pursued, touched, and *chosen* by men. So you know who the most passionate women in the world are, don't you? They're *single women* out to prove they're valuable!

Then we take this thing called marriage and put it around sex, and amusingly, sex becomes hard work. We don't have anything to prove anymore. We've passed the test. We have the ring on our finger, the Good Housekeeping Seal of Approval, and now all the mystique and challenge is gone.

Men marry anticipating sex like dessert every night or every other night, and women have moved on searching for depth and intimacy. Gabrielle Brown in her book *The New Celibacy* states, "People in this society know very well how to have sex. We know almost nothing about intimacy." Women are searching for romance and intimacy in marriage. I say to men when I speak to them, "If you want to move your wife toward the bedroom do almost *anything* kind except something sexual." Do you like that?

My husband is a great father. I watch him load my two little sons on bikes with a big bottle of pop and some sandwiches they've made, head out for a nine-mile bike ride, and I am moved toward him. I suggested this to a group of men recently when I spoke to them. When I returned in the evening to address them again, a handsome, tall man walked up to me and remarked, "Well, I've spent the entire afternoon playing with the neighbor's children in the backyard but nothing has happened yet."

Teach your husband some lessons in intimacy:

- Pour some hot tea, climb on his lap, and tell him your deepest feeling. You will feel closer to him, even if he doesn't open up and share back.
- Plan a fun evening out.
- Give him paper and a pencil and ask him to tell you three things he admires about you.
- Tell him you will do one thing today that he needs if he will return the favor.
- Listen to your husband with eye contact talk about anything.

Intimacy—experiencing life together in personal, meaningful ways is what draws women sexually after marriage. Disappointingly, men often seem just to want to get into bed and have sex.

3. *The third reported problem area is "What do I do when I find myself attracted to another man?"*

When I married Tom Ream I didn't think any man

could charm me again for a lifetime. I was in my office a few years back with a handsome executive who had come with his wife for counseling. I was seeing him alone that day, and he began to confess without his wife there of the many other women who had been in his life. I was listening seriously, when he looked at me directly and leaned forward and said, "To tell you the truth, Jan, I find you extremely attractive too." Now I've been propositioned before in therapy but never by someone I felt mutually attracted to. I was, first of all, dumbfounded but soon as I took a breath, flattered. I came home that night and told Tom first thing about this client who found me attractive. That seemed the safest thing to do!

I poured some hot tea and went into another room to ponder. So this is what happens to people. In a quiet office or at a dinner party you casually look across the room and your eyes find the eyes of a man looking at you like you haven't been looked at for ten years. My, how thrilling. You mean he finds me (little, old, plain *me*) *attractive*? It usually starts with talking. Many women never intend to end up in bed with someone besides their husband. But it's hard to be intimate with a man and not end up sexually entangled.

Now I knew I loved Tom very much. I knew I could never make this client happy. If Suzie and Josie and Beth and Diane hadn't, what made me think I could be the goddess he was looking for? Why then was I attracted? Most attractions erupt from deep, unresolved ego issues in our identities.

Growing up feeling ugly and unacceptable has not vanished away completely underneath my degrees, my smart clothes, and my roles as wife, mother, therapist, and speaker. There is still that piece of me I'm working on. My client had tapped in for a moment to those old messages deep inside me, and I suddenly wanted reassurance that I wasn't as bad as maybe a part of me still believed. But he was a human with the same flaw in his ego, selfishly looking to be reaffirmed. This wasn't love; it was selfishness.

You and I can respond one of three ways when we find ourselves attracted outside of marriage:

1. *Repress and deny we have ever felt such feelings and stand back and say, "Only bad people feel those things."*

2. *We can move with the feeling, pursue the person and the relationship.* Interpreting the feelings as representing something that surely must be "real" and beautiful. Getting caught in the hooks of "only I can make him happy."

3. *Begin to draw away and search out ourselves.* Ask the question, "Why is he becoming so attractive to me?" Are you looking for a medicine to restore your wounded ego? Is your marriage in shambles, and you're looking for an easy way out? Most people in unhappy marriages don't file for divorce unless they have already connected to someone else.

I've heard hundreds of stories from mistresses who say, "But I thought he really loved me." From wives and husbands who can never fully trust their mate again. From children who are disillusioned.

The answer for our broken, wounded egos should not be wrapped up in a continual search for someone out there to be enough to bandage our wound and make us happy. No human can ever be enough for that.

This story was told to me in therapy. "My husband had left with another woman twelve years ago. I hated her. I think I could have murdered her. But I began slowly putting the pieces of myself back together. A year ago our daughter married, and I ran into this other woman in my husband's life for the first time. I thought I would feel hate, but when I approached her, I was compelled to throw my arms around her. 'I'm so glad Richard has finally found someone to make him happy,' I said. This new wife backed up, and looking intently at me, replied, 'No, no one will ever make Richard happy.' "

Our sexuality is not wrapped up in belonging to a man. It's wrapped up in the love relationship we build with ourselves. In the development of our minds, bodies, friendships with men and women alike. Our learning to enjoy life and throw back our heads and laugh or weep.

The greatest underdeveloped commodity is a human life. So many women feel if they have grown to adulthood, married, conceived and delivered a child, done enough adult things, they have become "women." The sidewalks are full of undeveloped women walking around, looking for a man to make them complete or happy. Many of us are going to end up single, sooner or later. I hope we will throw ourselves into living and giving and developing further this incredibly unique person of *me*.

# 7.
# *Feelings*
## Jan

When Tre was six years old we were frantically looking for his Sunday shoes. Finally, stuffed in a corner of his closet underneath a sack of old clothes, we retrieved them. I, very uptight and tense, shoved him down on the bed and began to help him put them on. He began to cry, and said something about being dumb and I screeched back in a horrible voice, "You're not dumb." He looked at me and sobbingly responded, "I didn't say I was dumb. I said I *feel* dumb." A great distinction for a six-year-old child!

My mother used to say, "Puppy love is not real love, but it's real to the puppy." What we feel inside often is not realistic but it *authentically* seems to paint a real, truthful picture of what is actually happening. Learning to discern between what is real and what *feels* real is very important.

I remember the client who came to see me and proceeded to express how beautiful and gifted and talented she was. She was deeply disturbed that her friend didn't see her the same way. As she expounded on her physical beauty, I remember sitting there in astonishment and thinking to myself, *She's seeing things I can't possibly see.* Here was one person I've met who felt she was more exotic and exquisite than reality revealed.

The importance of feelings is that they give us messages about ourselves—even if our feelings are somewhat or extremely distorted. They still are rising up and being felt because there is a message you need to pay attention to. Very significantly our feelings tell us where we've been hurt. A message that tells us what we need or don't need. John Powell says, "Feelings are always telling us one of two things. They are telling us we need to stop doing something or they are telling us we need to start doing something." Sometimes we need to do both. A psychotherapist, Willard Gaylin, wrote a wonderful book titled *Feelings*, and he calls them our vital signs. The most authentic part of any human is what he *feels*.

I think there are three kinds of people:

1. *The people who are aware of their feelings and can use words to describe them.* If you were to ask them what they feel, they would ponder a moment and surface with some words to put some labels on what they are internally experiencing.

2. *There are the people who feel very deeply yet have little vocabulary to describe what they feel.* This does not mean, however, that they do not communicate their feelings. We can show many emotions without ever saying a word. We ignore or avoid people. We frown or smile. We stare at the floor when someone is talking to us. The trouble is until we can put into words what we feel, we cannot resolve our differences. Therefore, before anyone can *talk* about feelings, they need to become acquainted with all the different feelings one can feel and the words to represent those feelings. And *then* take the risk to express them in an appropriate way and in the right time and place.

3. *There are those who have become successful at not feeling what they don't want to feel.* They bury the feelings that would cause them distress and keep only conscious the feelings they are comfortable with. In other words, they feel selectively.

The most powerful motivators are *feelings*. The greatest good or worst evil begins with a feeling.

Feelings are what unite and connect people or drive them apart. Feelings are what breed marriage and divorce, success or failure, self-sacrifice or murder. Feelings are behind all our actions and behaviors.

In order for my feelings to be useful, *I must first of all become aware of what I feel.* I must be in touch with my feelings and have words to describe them.

*Second, I must have some loving, accepting, experienced person to share my feelings verbally with.* Feelings can only take on reality outside of ourselves. I come the closest to being real and alive when I am with someone who is understanding and kind, and lets me pour out my feelings into their hands, and they lovingly embrace them into their hearts. They neither frown nor look shocked nor tell me I'm wrong. They understand what it means to have feelings. They seem to immediately understand that feelings don't make me good or bad. They are the result of something I've experienced.

If I can lay my feelings out and find love and value and acceptance, I can then choose to do something productive with them. I can even choose to let them go.

I remember the day one of the dearest friends called to tell me she was on her way to buy a Louis Vuitton bag for her birthday. I had bought a Louis Vuitton purse a couple of years before, soon after moving to Shaker Heights, a suburb of prestige and considerable wealth. I had just started into private practice, and Tom was fresh out of graduate school, and we were struggling financially. I would go to the grocery store and dry cleaners and found myself feeling what I used to feel as a child growing up in Hawaii in a culture of Orientals and Islanders—inferior, too simple and plain—not earning enough respect from people around me. I knew the value of Louis Vuitton luggage because Ann had carried it for several years. On my birthday, she and I together had gone to Saks and bought me the cheapest bag they had, but nonetheless, it was blatantly *Louis Vuitton*. When I would go to the dry cleaners, I would plop my purse on the counter and (whether they did or not) I felt the women and men around me treated me with more respect. I'm amused at myself while I sit here writing this. That bag did not match anything else in my life, and I'm sure people saw me climb into my little banged-up Karmann Ghia and recognized the discrepancy. But at the time I felt worth more!

After talking to my friend about her proposed purchase, I hung up the phone that morning feeling a cloud settle over me. My same friend compares this feeling to a low-grade fever. Isn't she clever? Why did I feel so bad? I began to pursue the meaning behind this feeling. Sometimes it takes considerable time and effort to come to a truer, more honest understanding behind a feeling. A feeling always says more about us, you know, than it says about the other person.

I began to realize that for years this friend always admired the style and "class" (her word) of the way I dressed. That was not her forte. My fear, as I explored it, seemed to be one of losing this special place in her life. If she began to copy me, then what would she continue to admire? We were so alike in other ways. I think I also have to add that I had dressed like Ann every day for my first eighteen years of life, and that I had spent years thereafter trying to discover my own uniqueness. And even though I was still copying Ann, I certainly didn't want anybody copying me. (Smile.) I was shocked, and I will tell you, embarrassed and humiliated with these feelings. I knew that if I wasn't willing to be open with my friend and confess what I felt were absolutely hideous feelings, revealing my littleness in spirit, I would certainly communicate these feelings nonverbally. We were too close for me to hide them. I was petrified. Would this destroy a friendship? She must do what she felt was right. I would never ask her not to buy a purse like mine, but at least I would love her enough to communicate directly and openly instead of building a wall as I've done before in my life by trying to hide my true feelings.

When, over coffee, I poured out my smallness, she laughed and said, "I was only trying to keep up with you, so you don't get turned off by my simpleness and find me boring and dull. I am desperately trying to keep your approval." It was a time full of healing and cleansing, and I immediately became free of my fear.

I can't do this alone. Feelings poured out on paper have far more potential for growth than feelings unexpressed. However, if I have a tender, wise, accepting flesh-and-blood human to give them to, like my friend, I can then soar like the eagles. I can become free to live instead of bound and trapped inside with what I can't understand or accept.

A client of mine who is a heart surgeon walked out on his wife and four children. Two days later he called me, "I feel so inferior and inadequate and worthless. When it comes to dealing with people, I'm so ignorant." He was so sincere and honest, my heart connected to him.

Another client, minutes before our session ended said, "I've never told anyone this. I have terrible feelings about my baby. I wish she were dead."

Some of the greatest healing to take place in my office comes out of the courage to articulate what was being felt—the words being met with unconditional love and acceptance.

I went to see my good friend Harolyn Gilles, an M.D., for a physical before she left town. She examined me thoroughly. There was something I needed to tell her. I finally blurted out, sitting on the table with just a big sheet wrapped around me, "Harolyn, this takes more courage than I can tell you, but I have terrible feelings about my skin. I hate these freckles. Some of them are dark and stand out." She didn't look shocked or laugh or tell me I had better face the fact that I'm not a Raquel Welch. She simply looked at me warmly and said, "I've always seen you as beautiful, but if you want them gone we can take them off. You know, nearly everyone has some neurosis about their body. Yes, I do too." That moment changed my life. She had seen my skin, but it wasn't until I confessed my feelings that I really felt free from my body. If she wasn't horrified, I would no longer be either.

Life is a lot more than feelings, but without feelings there can be no life. Become acquainted with your feelings. Express your feelings and let yourself cry or laugh or even hurt. If your feelings would lead you to inappropriate behavior, begin to talk about them, share them, write them out on paper, and let them lead you to some new understanding of yourself and to alternate behavior. We cannot control our feelings, only our behavior.

If we can begin to face and acknowledge what we're feeling and begin to understand our feelings, we will find ourselves doing a lot less of the things we really don't want to do.

And when someone hands you a feeling—accept it with love. Don't try to rationalize it away. It can be a temptation to say, "Well, she was probably just tired and didn't mean to be gruff." That's a way of minimizing what is being felt. Don't offer advice, only your thoughts if they should ask. Listen with your eyes and your face and your heart. Accept what they hand you. Thank them for this priceless gift. Be vulnerable back. They are handing you the most precious thing you and I could ever receive. It may be a moment that will alter their lives and offer them new freedom to grow. And if we're loving enough, maybe they will hand us more.

# ann

"ann, you do NOT look ugly," will shouted over my tears.

"yes, honey, i do. i hate my hair. & i look fat in this dress," i cried.

will shook his head in disbelief, & headed for the garage to start the car. i grabbed my purse, the diaper bag (the baby was already in his car seat), & wiped the tears off my face as i stumbled out the door.

when we arrived at our friends' house, i bit my lower lip, deciding with all the willpower in me to smile & move beyond my selfish insecurities, & have fun. intellectually, i knew it was not how i looked that gave me value, or would determine whether the party was fun or not. on the feeling level, however, i was fragile & longing to be affirmed! & i KNEW i FELT UGLY.

after we had been visiting awhile, several women came to me & said, "ann, you look so beautiful. the colors in that dress really do something for you."

my feelings changed...from insecure & ugly, to relaxed & happy & relieved. i had the same dress on that i felt made me look fat. my hair was still limp. but the words of kindness changed completely my feelings. & the words needed to come from someone besides my husband.

my whole life i have struggled with feelings. the only moments i have significantly contributed to life were the times i moved *beyond* my feelings to action.

when i was a full-fledged runner & faithfully covered 10 to 12 miles a day, i felt my worst the 15 minutes before i got started. tired. sore. depressed. for those 10 to 15, i would argue with my feelings before i went out the door. had i given in to my feelings, i almost never would have run those miles every day. it would have been a shame because afterwards i always felt so good.

very few times, as a speaker, have i felt capable of walking out on stage. often, standing behind the curtains, i have said to myself, "i am a horrible speaker. i tell such simple stories. the trip was exhausting. my dress is wrinkled. 'God—i can't speak tonight!' "

then i would hear the m.c. introduce me, the cheers & applause. instantly pushing the ugly, discouraging feelings aside, i would boldly walk out under the spotlights, pray for God to somehow turn my weakness into something beautiful.

when i have stopped by a neighbor's with warm cookies, or run by the house of a bedridden patient just to visit, i have almost always had to move beyond my feelings to action. beyond feeling tired & discouraged & lazy to care for someone else.

when i miscarried a set of twins, i felt like the most defective, imperfect, inadequate woman in the world. i grieved as i had never grieved before. though i *knew* that only God Himself can help a woman carry a pregnancy full-term, i still struggled desperately not to let the feeling that i was a bad person drag me down.

my feelings are greatly influenced by circumstances. i feel good if the house is clean & pretty. if my hair comes out perfectly. if my makeup goes on right. if i am not 5 pounds too heavy. if someone has praised me. if my children & husband love me. if the bills are paid.

if any of these pieces go wrong, my feelings often erupt, leading me into disarray, sometimes into something so painful & dark that the whole world turns quiet, & waves of sadness roll over me. to be a whole person, i must learn to cover my feelings with faith. to not let circumstances control my moods, my happiness. to know that my feelings usually exaggerate the experiences, & make everything look much worse than it is...

jan has been my best friend in helping me cope with

my feelings. when i feel ugly, she tells me, via phone, how pretty she thinks i was the last time she saw me. when i tell her i feel so insignificant, she tells me of the latest person who mentioned to her that one of my books deeply affected her life. when i tell her i feel inferior to her, she says she understands. that she's lived with those feelings all her life.

if i could not talk about my feelings to someone, as rational or irrational as they might be, i do not know how i could make it. it is so vulnerable to tell my feelings to you. to feel safe enough. to know you will not laugh or minimize them, but help me work through them.

most people i know try to talk me out of my feelings.

"ann, you should not be too sad about miscarrying those twins. look at the beautiful, little boys you have."

"ann, you should not feel depressed about moving to idaho. at least you have a strong, handsome husband. what more do you want."

a lot of my feelings may not be real, but they are very real to *me*. i need someone to love me enough to empathize with them, after i am honest enough to share them. i need courage to discern the difference between what is real & what is not. i need faith in a loving God to carry me above & beyond my feelings to the bigger picture. the long haul of life.

# 8.
# Change

ann

from the first night of my marriage i started sleeping on the left side of the bed. it just began that way, & i felt comfortable with it. about six months later, i crawled into bed & will said, "honey, let me sleep on your side. i think i could do better over there."

"no-o-o-o-o...i'm used to this side now."

"please, ann...i want to."

before i knew what was happening, he rolled over me, with his pillow, & balanced on the narrow piece between me & the edge of the bed. there was no moving this 6'2½", 190-lb. man.

it may seem insignificant to you, but at that moment in my life, i remember feeling such internal rage & helplessness. will was not going to budge. that was obvious. & i was stuck on the right side of the bed where i did not feel comfortable.

*change* is so difficult. it represents the unfamiliar. the less secure & safe pieces of life. some people are more adaptable to change. some more rigid. as much as i hate to admit it, i probably fall into the more rigid category.

i got out of bed. pulled on shorts & running shoes & headed out into the black night to run off my frustration & anger. i cried. & angrily told God how i felt about will anderson (i was not very kind!). exhausted after 6 miles, i fell into the right side of the bed...the side farthest from the bathroom...& dropped off to sleep, feeling very unhappy, strange & uncomfortable with the change.

now, after 3½ years, i love that side of the bed. several times since, will has suggested we "switch again" for "variety." believe me, i refuse. one bed change is enough! (smile.)

one of the hardest things in life, i think, is dealing with change. from what i observe, it is something people are having to deal with constantly. even in the later years of life, when they are old.

the other night, i was in pennsylvania to address a pregnancy-crisis-center dinner. jan had flown in to be with me because the next day we were doing an all-day women's seminar in a town 20 minutes away. for years, i had been the leader of the two of us. the more aggressive, self-assured, confident one. jan often became quiet when we were together & let me carry the conversation.

seated around a large, circular table at the front of the room, jan & i had been placed, not side by side, but with several people between us. it was amusing to me as i watched jan. she was so animated. laughing. relaxed. freely conversing with the different ones around the table. i was rather quiet, in the background. smiling sweetly. letting her carry the table...as she had allowed me to do for years.

i spoke, autographed books. we slipped away to our hotel rooms where the nurse was watching our 3 little boys.

"jan, everything has changed. our roles have completely reversed. you are now the confident, secure, aggressive leader. i am the quiet, unsure sister."

i felt amused by the reality. i felt pain, too. so much in the last three years has changed me. jan lives in the cleveland suburban area where there are many smart women's shops & sophisticated stores. her clothes are beautiful & up-to-date. classy. i live in a community of 40,000, & there are two lovely dress shops for women, but only two, & with a size 4, i often cannot find just what i want.

i have been pregnant, so waiting, knowing i will be into maternity clothes. then, another miscarriage, & left with the clothes i have had hanging in my closet for several years.

jan, for years would call & tell me how sad she felt. or inferior to me. not-as-good-as. for years, i did not understand. i was self-assured. God & i were changing the world. there was nothing i felt God & i, together, could not do. her struggle was beyond my comprehension.

change has brought a perspective to me. the change to idaho after boston. of marriage after 35 years of singleness & being in control of my own life. of seeing jan suddenly capable of doing things i, for the first time, could not keep up with. like having babies. of flying in to cleveland to see her, & discovering that, for the first time, she was the one with all the sharp clothes, the newest styles. i looked like the small-town girl. it jarred my sense of security. my identity.

there are some people i know who cannot accept change. they do not take better jobs, or promotions because they fear what change will bring. of living across the country from family. of not having all the same faithful friends one is used to. of having to learn new topography. new streets. new neighbors.

change is hard. change is challenging. but...change, if one lets it, brings a creative flow of feelings & experiences that can give life more quality.

maybe change has made me less self-confident in areas. less self-assured. it has taught me compassion because it has forced me to feel more authentic human emotions. it has put me more in touch with the hurting world. it has given me the opportunity to step aside & let jan take the lead, & know the fun & joy of that. it has forced me away from my tendency to be rigid. narrow. guarded.

for eleven months, i had taylor, my firstborn, to myself. it was wonderful pouring all my energy & creativity into his small, miraculous, beautiful life. now i have my secondborn. another son. what change! i must share my attention with 2 babies now. must learn to be fair with two in terms of my time & output. must learn to have enough left over for will, my husband, because it takes so much more energy having two babies than one.

today, jan runs more than i do. (i remember when she & tom would clock me for 20-mile runs.) someday, she may weigh less, & i, more. friends may, who were once poor & struggling while we were succeeding, rise & fly beyond me. those who were my followers may some day become my leaders.

frankly, i must be humble enough, & vulnerable

enough, to say change is hard...sometimes very threatening ...very frightening...change does not go away. it forces some kind of response from us.

i have heard stories of how a spouse, in a marriage, changes dramatically for the good, & the other spouse loses a sense of his/her role. we get used to living with an overeater. one who weighs a lot more. we get used to being "better than" in our thinking. "stronger." when suddenly we lose some superior status, we get scared & unsure of our worth.

everybody is always changing, & our security is usually wrapped up in how we relate to all those people around us. change is always forcing us to relate differently. change lifts one person up & brings another down.

for me, so much of the new wholeness i have is a result of surviving many life experiences. i've been up. i've been down. i know success. i know failure. i have spoken to 40,000 people at one rally, & received a thundering, standing ovation. i have gone to another auditorium where they expected 20,000 & 1,000 showed & all i could see were 19,000 empty seats. at one time, i took 21 people as my guests to Israel. a few years later, there wasn't enough money to buy them each a small Christmas present. i was dean of women at a small college & a lovely, young woman sought my advice. five years later, she was the dean, sitting behind my desk, & i had moved on to something else.

it is so easy to get used to a certain role. a certain city. one kind of car...of weather. to seeing someone fat instead of skinny. strong instead of weak. when any of these change, i begin to compare myself to the change. do i feel as good as before? or worse than? often, i panic.

when my little sons start asserting themselves more, i must learn to let them do that. when they become less dependent on me, i want to cheer them on to their own self-reliance & not worry about whether i am as important to them as i used to be. if will wants to pick up & move to africa for three years (or whatever), & he really believes this is God's will, i want to be brave & open enough to say *yes.* to stretch my life. our circle of friends. to offer our children fresh adventures.

change means age. & wrinkles. & more gray hairs. my

mother always said, "i want to look my age. to be who i am. to make it a thing of beauty."

she does not dress like a teen-ager. she has a lot of gray streaked through the black. she somehow seems to understand that change does not affect her value. only her response to it can do that.

as i write this chapter, i feel such deep emotion. it seems i have had almost a brutal amount of change in the last few years & experienced some deep emotions of fear & insecurity & uncertainty. i have felt weakness overcome all the places in me i thought were strong. yet, saying *yes* to the changes has developed a tenacity of spirit...a courage...a humility i could not know otherwise. wholeness cannot come without it.

# Jan

I flew into Allentown, Pennsylvania, a few days ago to be a keynote speaker with Ann for a group of women. We met at the hotel. I was traveling with my youngest son, nine months, and she joined me with her two sons, an eleven-month-old and a five-day-old-newborn and a nurse traveling with her. We piled our suitcases, squirming babies, boxes of diapers, and formula into our two adjoining rooms. Then we attempted to clean up and head for the evening banquet, stumbling over crawling babies, dirty diapers, and toys strewn across the floor.

When the banquet was finally over and we had shaken the last hand, we wearily headed back up to our hotel room. Ann looked at me as we climbed the steps to our second-floor room and said, "You have become an 'Ann' and I've gone to being a 'Jan.'" I was startled. "You walked into that banquet, sat down, and with great confidence began to smile and talk. I sat there quite quiet with not much to say," she continued. I was amazed by the picture she painted of me—a picture I was not at all aware of. When had I crossed over from all those feelings I had lived with for years and years? Feelings of insignificance and inferiority to Ann. When had I moved to a place where I really do have a sense of my own personhood? For all of my life—a seeming eternity—I had lived smiling on the outside and feeling crippled and ugly and inferior on the inside. For the first time I consciously became aware that change in me had indeed occurred. My feelings around myself had changed and it was altering my expressions and behaviors on the outside.

As I sit and write these thoughts, I'm keenly aware

that change has also been occurring in Ann. Over a period of months and maybe the last three years, she has somewhere crossed over from feeling she was strong, in control, capable of absolutely any phenomenal task she felt inspired to accomplish to feeling little control and overpowered by forces beyond all the effort and energy and brains she could expend. Maybe she had to lose some strength and confidence for me to find some!

Regardless of all scientific ingenuity and deep, determined effort, she has not been able to carry a child to term and deliver a baby. She has run into an immovable mountain. Perhaps seeing her seeming indestructible self-confidence finally weakened by this equally immovable mountain of infertility is what has brought her closer to me. I have at last seen her capable of experiencing the kind of inferiority I carried strapped on my back for years, and I must admit—seeing she is not all-powerful has made me feel less weak.

It's a temptation, I think, to believe that we are "good or bad," "weak or strong," according to some unique, innate gifts (or lack of gifts) we have been blessed or damned with from our Creator. The more I observe life, I think it is rather the result of what we have experienced and are still experiencing with life. If I'm in the middle of life and it's going positively, I can think I'm strong and unusual and gifted—different from those struggling. But by the time life is over we will all have had a taste of all emotions—grief and joy, success and failure, humiliation and pride, superiority and inferiority, significance and insignificance.

Wholeness is wrapped up in having experienced all the different places life can bring. Leo Buscaglia says, "At the end of life at least be able to say, 'I have lived.' "

I have become close to a beautiful, clever woman who owns a smart dress shop in a sophisticated suburb. Before I left town last week I called and told her I was coming to her shop. I have always been a "follower." Whatever Ann wore I would go and search through stores trying to find something similar. For years I didn't have as much money to spend, and so whatever I did buy was a cheaper copy. When we would meet out-of-town, my first painful moment was watching her waltz off the plane—a gorgeous, chic outfit of the latest fashion, a smile reaching clear across her face—her hair flowing, a picture of confidence, and definite superiority. Then we would get to our hotel room and I would steel myself and open up her hanging bag to see again how superior she really was. I might have gone out and bought something I thought was smart looking before catching my plane or meeting her. However, one look in her hanging bag would send waves of confirmation of my inferiority as I would view her clothes. She always seemed to know better what was in. Having been a follower for so many years always made clothes shopping very painful. I had trouble making decisions and feeling secure and confident about my choices.

Jan McClennan gave me a warm hug when I walked into her shop. I have to admit, I felt drained before I got there. Exposing my body to this sharp lady was my first uncomfortableness and then it was (always has been) so difficult for me to believe she could find anything that would really look good on me. For two hours I stood in a dressing room while she brought me outfits. I did not have to look through one rack of clothes. She tied belts and scarves, and she and her saleswomen gave me so much affirmation and approval. There were moments I think I had most of the clothes in the shop in my dressing room. Jan worked fervently, bringing me outfits and carrying them away. She has great flair, and by the time we were done, I had fallen in love with much more than I could afford. She even at one point took off her own dress to see how it looked on me. And I tried it on while she stood in her bra and panties.

She should have received a gold medal that day for all the love and warmth and beauty and confidence she wrapped around me. Finally she brought me a cup of coffee and whisked the things I had chosen and made them affordable for me to buy. I drove home that day overwhelmed by her kindness and the gorgeous clothes I could not possibly have found in any department store if I had spent one week shopping, eight hours a day.

When I met Ann and we pulled out our outfits to wear—I was amazed that we both had the longer "in" skirts and for the first time I felt no pain of inferiority—only equality. Why didn't God put a Jan McClennan in my life years ago? I could have missed all those years of struggle over my body and appearance. But then I would have missed experiencing a vital side to life—to wholeness. And if Ann hadn't moved to Idaho—out of the mainstream of fashion—she would have missed a vital side also.

Change offers us a much broader perspective of ourselves. It gives us a taste of many perspectives, experiences, and feelings. Who I think I am is altered over and over again in a lifetime by what new experience I've had—by some new place I find myself in, often not by choice.

Life is changing for us all the time. My children grow up, my husband dies or leaves me, I lose my job, or am offered a position of a lifetime, I'm the only good pianist in our church and suddenly a new couple comes to town and our church, and she's from the Julliard School of Music.

Change, as a matter of fact, is both comforting and humbling, depending on where I am today. But it takes change to reveal to us who we are and who we aren't. Change keeps bringing into focus that life doesn't have favorites. It keeps challenging us to face who we are and are not. Every change gives us an opportunity to become more whole—to see more clearly how alike we all are. Today, I know where I am. I also know where I've been. I'm not sure what is ahead, only that it will be a challenge for me to keep holding on loosely to where I am and what I have, for eventually it will be gone and I will be holding some new place in my hands. The biggest challenge is to see it all as useful—if I will only allow it to lead me closer to myself and truth and you and God.

AFTER A WHILE*

After a while you learn
The subtle difference between
holding a hand
and chaining a soul
and you learn
that love doesn't mean
leaning
and company doesn't always mean
security.

*Copyright Veronica Shoffstall 1971. Used by permission.

And you begin to learn
That kisses aren't contracts and
presents aren't promises
and you begin to
accept your defeats
with your head up and your eyes ahead
with the grace of a woman
not the grief of a child
and you learn
To build all your roads on today
because tomorrow's ground is
too uncertain for plans
And futures have a way of falling down
in mid-flight
After a while you learn
That even sunshine burns
if you ask too much
So you plant your own garden
and decorate your own soul
instead of waiting for someone to bring you flowers
And you learn
that you really can endure
that you really are strong
and you really do have worth
And you learn
And you learn
with every goodbye
You learn…

# 9.
# *Depression & Fear*
## Jan

I think I could write a volume on the emotion of fear. It's the most familiar of all the emotions I have experienced.

Gerald Jampolsky, author of *Love Is Letting Go of Fear*, takes the viewpoint that we respond to all humans either out of fear or out of love.

I believe we can look at what we feel and come to understand better what we have experienced. I am convinced I encountered a lot of pain because I am prone to the emotion of fear. Fear was created to protect us—to keep us from returning to someone or some situation that could hurt us again.

A few weeks ago a good friend of ours completed his course-work for his Ph.D. and passed his orals. I was amazed by my own smallness and the consuming fear I felt. I wanted to do what I travel cross-country encouraging others to do—celebrate with him—I wanted to brag and tell him how great an achievement I felt it was. But I was paralyzed, I was afraid—afraid it would and already did once and for all confirm his superiority over us. I know I'm a therapist and I hate to admit my humanity, but I felt fearful of this new place in our friend's life. Not fearful of his success but fearful of being insignificant again, of feeling him project superiority over those of us less educated. I felt grief over these feelings of mine. I deep down believe he needs my affirmation as much as I need his.

I honestly wanted to give him a standing ovation, but my lips were paralyzed shut. The words I wanted and should have said were trapped inside my throbbing fear and pain of being inferior. All I was able to do was commit to myself that I would somehow move beyond my fear, I would let some time pass and strive for a better sense of my own worth. I would, someday, belatedly, extend my joy for his success. In a few weeks, we're to have dinner with this couple, and I hope I can confess this crippledness in my humanity and extend a round of applause. I owe him that. He's been a great friend.

Fear is alive and well in the lives of many people. They confess it to me daily in my office. One gifted, lovely woman I worked with told me of several friendships she had annihilated because she became fearful of her friends becoming better and stronger than she was. Strewn behind her were many wonderful people. Hurt and rejected (and probably with no idea as to why they had suddenly been cast out). And my lovely friend continues to find herself alone and trapped inside this mass of fear and pain.

Unhealthy fear seems to stem out of our personal sense of weakness and inadequacy. It's crippling and so destructive to our relationships with others and our love for ourselves.

Depression is another "state of being" we have to accept as a part of our crippled humanity. Some depression is internalized—a darkness that seems to consume one with no apparent external cause. However, most depression is what we call *exogenous* or depression which stems from external circumstances going on in our lives. It seems to occur with change and the loss of something or someone we've grown comfortable with. Our minds want to jump to the great losses such as divorce, death, job loss, and illness. But there are many smaller losses that create some degree of depression—age lines beginning to form around our eyes—the loss of being invited to a desired party—the loss of the sale of a house you've been working on. Life is full of losing, and with the losses come the anger and hurt toward ourselves, others, or the situation God and life have handed us.

It's so important to keep directing our energies toward what may seem like a small amount of strength or power that still lies within our hands. *What tiny effort this moment can I exert to bring some of what I need or want back into my life?* needs to be asked. *How can I keep you from continuing to hurt me? How can I feel better about myself today?* We must see ourselves with the help of God as having the power to bring the change we need. The *blamers* have no hope of moving from sickness to health.

My only pathway to freedom will come with my picking up my body and energies and thoughts and assuming responsibility for my own well-being day after day, month after month, until the situation changes. We can kick and scream at all the hurts and disappointments, and it won't change a thing.

Fear is usually a big part of depression. I think that two of the greatest fears women face is the fear of failure and the fear of rejection. They so often seem to go together. When women lose a husband to another woman, they report with screaming agony, "I wasn't good enough. I was a failure as a wife and now he's rejected me with no second chance to succeed—to redeem myself—to prove I am worthwhile." One of my beautiful clients, recently divorced, wrote me, "I hate being considered a mistake in someone's life. I suppose the sense of rejection and failure will be even greater if I don't make any effort to go on with life. No one likes a failure. Everyone for sure will desert me or feel sorry for me. Yeah, I feel like a failure but I'm determined to beat it most of the time." This woman is a survivor. She doesn't throw her shovel into the sandbox and quit. She recognizes that quitting and becoming bitter will lead her to deeper despair and hopelessness. It's one thing to fail and get a second chance, but to fail and be rejected both is enough to bury most of us.

Ten years ago I was asked to be on a team that would travel cross-country speaking to teachers. I was asked to address some possible approaches to dealing with hyperkinetic children, and I was excited by this unique opportunity. I had become pregnant with our first child but was determined to follow through on the tour. We met in Dallas, Texas, for our first big convention. I spoke to the six hundred professionals in that group, and the response seemed phenomenal. Men and women grabbed my hand and thanked me. With smiles of pleasure, the man in charge reported that I was "terrific." I boarded my plane with a great sense of "mission accomplished."

Our next seminar was a month away. I went into the office one morning to see a client and found a letter from the man in charge of the team.

"Dear Jan, Thank you for your great contribution. Some of the ladies on the committee feel a pregnant woman should not be on the platform so we are removing you from your assignment with us." I was stunned. What in the world was I going to tell everybody—my mother who was so proud of me? My heart picked up rapidly and I could almost hear it pulsating. Fear and humiliation and fury poured throughout my whole body. What did he mean, I was "removed from my assignment"? I knew there was more to it than pregnancy. My word, this was a group of mostly *women*! My first feelings were "I'm a failure and I'm being rejected." My lifelong fear had become a reality. I had a choice: I could grieve and accept this ultimatum silently; or I could at least call this man and represent myself. He was in the Caribbean at the time. (I would have called China.)

"I just received your letter. I'm shocked and deeply hurt. I know there is more than pregnancy involved here—what is it? What were you unhappy with? I feel I have failed and I have been given no chance to redeem myself. The thing I've feared all my life has finally happened—I've not been good enough and now you are rejecting me." I insisted he state the issues. I agreed I could improve. Interestingly, what I believe was operating on his side was fear also. Fear he might be criticized, not be "good enough" himself as the leader. I ran and cried and suffered that day. Once again this terror of failure and rejection I've fought all my life to escape was consuming me. What would Tom think of me? My mother?

It all worked out! They insisted I come back, and I did. I understood better what they wanted, and it ended up being a tremendous learning experience for all of us. Thank God for those who are willing to give someone a second chance.

Even if they had not invited me back, I had at least faced this man with my deepest feelings and perceptions. Not blaming but seeking truth that somehow lay buried under the ultimatum in his letter. There is a strength and peace that comes from simply reminding someone you are a feeling person who is worthy of being heard. As I confronted this man lovingly, I was amazed by how out of proportion my sense of failure had become. One of my favorite Scriptures in the Bible is "You shall know the truth, and the truth shall make you free" (John 8:32). The more truth I discovered through our conversations, the clearer the whole picture became. It was not nearly as deadly as it had seemed, and I found strength to work through it. My phone call to the Caribbean that morning (probably cost me a hundred dollars) was the one resource of help I held in my hand to bring me to truth and the beginning of healing. Together we struggled through to an understanding that was better for both of us. We negotiated our differences to meet the needs of all.

Fear and depression plague every woman I know—those in lovely homes and beautiful clothes—professionals and highly educated—housewives and mothers. Our response needs to be, "I can grow through this. I must fight to survive—to face the truth—to represent myself—to believe I am still good." We need to remember, "This too shall pass." Eventually we can swim our way to the other side of the despair and be more complete than ever before.

# ann

it was Good Friday. will & i were driving to boise to meet our friends, chuck & patty, for lunch. turning on the radio, i heard a man say, "it's friday—BUT SUNDAY IS COMING!"

for 3½ years it has been friday in my life. i have had moments of such pain & depression i feared i would never laugh again. it has been this quiet blanket that covers me. that folds me in a darkness & a despair that is so silent...so illusive...that at times i do not even identify it as depression. only as weariness. with no energy. no sparkle. no strength for living.

moving to a new piece of the world which was completely unfamiliar to me. where i did not know who i was. where i did not feel safe. where i had no one to confide in. being in the hospital 9 times in one year with pregnancy-related problems. miscarriages. getting older & older. watching my body age. new little wrinkle lines. even if no one else notices, i do. running no longer was a big part of my life. doctors did not want it to be. though i am very thin, it only deepened my depression. everywhere i look, the word is "fitness," & i have never felt less fit.

it's friday...BUT SUNDAY IS COMING.

before you finish reading *Struggling for Wholeness*, you will think jan & i have something terrible & awful for skin. if you saw us on the street, you probably would never even think we have freckles on our legs or shoulders. they are small & unnoticeable & basically insignificant...*except to us!* they are exaggerated in our thinking, but the defectiveness we feel is real.

about five weeks ago, after my last miscarriage, i was

feeling very sad. never have i felt so defective around my body. will was at a meeting of some kind one evening, & i got the idea to do something about the tiny freckles on my thighs. going to the bathroom, i found this little bottle of acid that a dermatologist had given me 10 years ago, & i proceeded to dot the little spots with acid. it was hard for me to remember when to apply the alcohol, & by the time i had done what i thought was right, my legs were burning & stinging, & it did not seem to go away.

for several days, i tried to hide my legs from will. it never crossed my mind they would not heal. i just thought it best to let them improve as much as possible before he saw them, for i predicted he would not be pleased. like tom, jan's husband, he loves the splashes of freckles.

while i was crawling out of the bathtub one morning, he walked in & the most shocked, horrified look crossed his face...

"ann, what have you done?"

"honey, i was so depressed. so sad. i wanted to feel better so i took some acid & tried to burn off my freckles. but maybe i got too much on..."

at first he laughed, shaking his head. "i have married a crazy woman."

then he got upset. it was so beyond his rational train of thought. so outrageous in his male logic. he was angry that i would do such a "ridiculous" thing. (the plastic surgeon said will needed a few more years living with a woman. he would understand it better down the road.)

"ann, your legs are going to scar!"

"then i'll go to grant [plastic surgeon] & see what he can do. oh, will, please do not reject me. please be kind. i wanted to do a good thing. something to make me feel better. now everything is even worse."

i took vitamin e. spread the oil on the little spots. suffered, in silence, with stinging pain that would not go away. felt more trapped in my defective body than ever because i could no longer wear shorts. had always to make sure the upper part of my legs were covered when someone came to the door.

finally, i went to the plastic surgeon. in tears. in trepidation.

"ann, you really did do a job on yourself. second-degree burns. that must have hurt! well...i have good news & bad news. they will heal & go away. but not for maybe a year. it will probably take that long for the pink color to go out of the spots."

it's been only 6 weeks, & a year seems forever. it's almost summer, & it means no sun. no shorts. no swimming. everytime i go to the bathroom, or pull on hose, or get undressed, i see all those pink spots on my upper legs, & i would give *anything* to have freckles back.

will smiles over it now. hugs me & still shakes his head. "you see, honey, when you try to undo the good that God does, it all goes wrong."

he is right. but it is too late. i cannot go back. i must wait it out. though i have pretty clothes, & it is all hidden, & no one knows, i know. it is a bad secret, & i hate bad secrets.

so much of my depression has come from doing things in weak, fragile moments that i cannot undo. cannot change. must suffer the consequences. must carry the memories.

today, i have a strong, exciting husband. two beautiful, gentle, magical babies. nine best-selling books. BUT I AM SO SAD. i have a new defect: my legs. a whole year for the spots to go away seems forever. there is even a dark cloud in my mind that keeps saying, "the surgeon says they will disappear, but what if they don't?"

> The world is full of *what ifs*.
> *what if* i never marry?
> *what if* i never succeed?
> *what if* i never have a baby?
> *what if* i never graduate?
> *what if* she never recovers from the accident?
> *what if* they sue me?
> *what if* someone finds out that i'm—?
> *what if...what if...what if...*

the fear & depression created in us by those two simple words can be so crippling.

well...it's friday, but sunday is coming!

after traveling the world & meeting thousands of people, i know depression is a real part of living. some people are better at masking it than others. at denying it. but everyone, everywhere has experienced it.

disciplining my mind to concentrate on the positives has helped me. when i was a child, my mother would say, "most of life goes on in your head, not your heart. you *choose* to be happy or unhappy. to see the good or the bad." that is hard work. it takes as much discipline as running 10 miles. it is a choice. determinedly, focus on the positives.

something else that has helped me in depression is to move beyond my pain & reach out to someone else. i remember one day feeling so depressed i could hardly roll over in bed. there was no energy left in me for anything. somehow, i wanted to stay under the covers & just die there.

with sheer, gut determination, i rolled out of bed. put clothes on my body with every thread of strength i could muster. stopped at a grocery store & bought two sacks full for a lonely, old widower. i sang to him, & visited with him, & left groceries on his kitchen table. there were a couple other people i thought of. one, a teen-age boy who was so socially crippled. picking up two cokes, i sat on the front steps with him & let him tell me his problems.

it was dark by the time i returned home. nothing had changed in my life. all the problems still existed. but i was light-hearted. the terrible weight of darkness & weariness was gone. i saw a streak of hope stretch across the sky. new energy surged in me.

depression can be so selfish, so crippling. give your life away to others, over & over & over & the black, dark places will become lighter. refuse, stubbornly, to let it block out the needs of others. to encase you in a tunnel of self-doubt & greed.

& remember...always...

it's friday...

the cross. pain. loss.

BUT SUNDAY IS COMING.

sunrise. fresh beginnings. surprises.

# 10.

# The Still, Small Voice: Conscience

## Jan

"Come Tre. Grab your lunch box. Nash. Get your jacket. We've got to get out of here!" I screeched. I picked up my twenty-pound baby with snowsuit and blanket, diaper bag, purse, and briefcase—and dragged myself to the car.

Mother, wife, therapist, speaker, daughter, friend, that's a lot to keep up with for a thirty-nine-year-old woman. Some days I feel *very* old.

I was a professional woman when I married. I went back to graduate school and had been a private therapist for two years before our first son was born.

As children the only goal Ann and I really had was to grow up and become wives and mothers. I don't think the possibility of professionalism ever crossed my mind. I assumed that upon completion of college, I would be engaged and marry and settle down into homemaking. It was a brutal awakening when I found myself still single upon graduation day, and there were no prospective husbands in view. I was forced out into the world to make it much to my disgust.

My first year of private practice I used to sit in the office and pray for clients. I had no children. Just Tom and hours of free, boring time.

Today I have three children and more clients wanting in than I can see and far too many speaking demands. I rise in the middle of the night and go into my little sons' room. I kiss Nash's closed eyes and whisper God's care over him. Then I climb to the top bunk, pull the covers up under Tre's chin, kiss his fingers and plead for God's wisdom over my life. I pick

Christian up out of his crib, snuggle his limp, sleeping body next to mine and rock him a few minutes and put him back to bed. Am I really a good mother and wife? Am I succeeding at the only thing I ever aspired to as a child? Am I listening to the inner voice?

A good friend of mine said to me the other day, "All I ever wanted growing up was a degree by my name, B.S. or M.S. Instead I married young, began having children, and the only degree I have is a M.O.M."

Isn't life a paradox? So imperfect. Often so different from what we expect and try to shape it into.

To write this I've left Tre and Nash with Tom and some wonderful women. Brought Christian and have had to farm him out because I just can't write without total quietness. Are my children, as Ann said, going to grow up insecure while I'm sitting over here writing on wholeness? It reminds me of all the people who are in marriage who want out and those who are out wanting in. A great dilemma for women today is "What is really right for me to do?"

Women report to me that their ministers are telling them to stay home until their children grow up and then they can "find themselves." I had a client once who tested out as a genius. She hated staying home all the time but felt guilty developing her brain and fighting upstream against extremist Christians. So instead she had affairs to add excitement to her life.

There are women who are completely fulfilled at home. My baby-sitter, Cathy, is like this. She's creative, a great cook, interested in a lot of things, and involved but a full-time homemaker. I call her my children's surrogate mother. She's fabulous, and I envy her contentment without having to make a statement to the world.

I do therapy two days a week, travel to speak twice a month six to seven months out of the year, and I wonder how you women who work full-time live long lives and stay out of mental institutions. I can't imagine working five days a week and still having the laundry, cleaning, grocery shopping, and cooking to come home to.

I don't think there are any simple answers to this dilemma. Probably, whatever side of the fence you end up on, the grass is going to look greener on the other side. We must listen to the inner voice.

I think we must strive for balance. My inner sense of peace disintegrates the most quickly when I've taken on too many clients and speaking engagements, and I am not with my children for long stretches of time. There is a screaming, kicking rebellion that finally walks me to my phone, and I clear some time on my calendar. My greatest personal tragedy would be if I should help the world and my own children and marriage not receive what they need from me.

I do believe that every woman needs to establish a piece of life for herself outside of her marriage and motherhood. "A sense of this is who I really am." Jan Ream does not equal a mother. Jan Ream does not equal a wife. Jan Ream equals a person, her unique gifts and abilities, her own viewpoints and ideas and feelings. Jan Ream, the person, is also a mother, and a wife, a therapist. These are the roles she plays. For some women being a mother is all they want. That may leave them feeling insignificant and not important when their children leave home.

The Bible tells us to "love your neighbor as yourself." I cannot be very effective as a wife and mother if I don't first know and love me. Then I have something to give my children and husband and you.

My life has led me along a different path than I expected. I am here and must pray and struggle to work out the best plan—not a perfect plan—for me and for those I have committed myself to. Some days I do a lot better than others. But this still small voice becomes louder and louder when I'm not being true to my deepest convictions. Listen to *your* still, small voice.

# ann

my husband says that most of the time we are too busy to listen, but when we are quiet enough to hear that "still, small voice," we can be changed in some of the most remarkable ways.

it was one night late in the bunk house, as will was overseeing his & his father's large seed potato ranch, that he began to feel very alone & far away from the exciting things in the world. that still, small voice said, "become a man of prayer…pray for a woman of God's choosing…"

for ten years, at the end of a dirt road in dubois, idaho, my husband did that though he said there were only 12 exciting single women in the entire county, & 6 were under 6 & over 60. in a remarkable story, God brought will anderson, potato farmer, & ann kiemel, boston author, together.

only when one is in touch with one's soul…with the truest, inner feelings…& heeds them…only then can we live in peace with ourselves.

jan is a therapist, a wife, a mother of three, a speaker, a writer. it is easy for her schedule to become overloaded. crowded. for her family to have too small a piece of her. many times i hear her tell of canceling dates & clearing her calendar because of a deep sense of truth that says, "slow down…uncomplicate."

when i married, i was making ten to twelve appearances a month. traveling five out of seven days a week. after moving to idaho, i began to cut back, but became more & more uneasy about the time i was still spending away from will on the road. as i said *yes* to the inner voice, & *no* to the calls coming in from my agent for speaking, peace came to me. more harmony with will. balance.

one of my greatest struggles has been with my conscience. to avoid compromise...knowing some things are not quite right, but to keep fudging anyway.

in dating men before i married, there were so many nights when i wish i had drawn the line...halted the action ...before i did. granted, compared to most women, i would probably appear angelic & puritanical, but i knew, for me, i was not true to my deepest sense of wholeness. of what i wanted to live & die by. there would have been so much less frustration & guilt had i been true to that.

once i was invited to speak in a huge coliseum with a world-renowned celebrity as co-speaker. they offered me a handsome sum of money. when they notified me of the date, it was during a time i had planned to be with my parents. we had built lovely adventures & much anticipation around those days, & to speak instead of keeping my commitment to my parents created a big dilemma.

my parents had loved me long before i was in demand as a speaker. had stood beside me all my life. bred into me my values. was i to disappoint them just for a big sum of money & more glamour? i heard the quiet voice. i had the most meaningful time with my dad & mother. there were no regrets. to this day, i have not met that famous man, but i am sure i could not tell you where the money might have gone. my seventy-seven-year-old father had a heart attack a couple of months ago. we almost lost him. i cherish every memory.

not always have i obeyed the quiet voice. many times, i have chosen to ignore it. always, insensitivity to my deepest, truest heart led me to compromise...the quality of life i longed for was lost. the quiet voice is there on big issues, & small ones. treasure it. listen daily, hourly for it. say *yes* to it. it is our only guarantee of holding on to truth & balance & thus, peace.

# 11.
# *Pain*
## Jan

When I was a little girl, I not only had freckles, I had a few moles on my back. (Yes, I'm writing about *freckles* again!) To write this for the world to read is very risky stuff, and yet somehow as I pen it I realize how whole I've become to be able to reveal to you a part of me more painful than I've ever confessed before. My father, an old-time Holiness preacher, led me to believe that if I prayed for anything and had enough faith, God would do what I had asked. I would go to bed at night and work up all the faith I could, and then ask God for a miracle. "Please, God, when I awake in the morning, may I find flawless skin." But morning after morning I awoke with my freckles and moles, not sure if I hadn't had enough faith or whether God just didn't love me enough to grant my request. I felt trapped in a body I could not live with.

After many years of suffering I reached inside myself and pulled out enough courage to call a doctor and get all my moles removed and some of my freckles. I said, "There, that's the end of that struggle," and went out to buy all the slinky, backless nightgowns I could afford, and would crawl into bed by myself and believe that some day, when I married, I would be able to expose my body to a man.

When Tre was four years old (a child who had been born flawless), one morning while washing his hair I noticed up under his hairline a couple of flat moles or freckles I wasn't sure. I was paralyzed. Surely, God would not hand me back an issue I had already agonizingly grappled with, but He did. I screamed inside. How could I face this issue again? I immediately called a dermatologist, made an appointment, and once again walked through the pain I thought I had buried forever.

As a high school senior, I sat in the school auditorium watching a play and quite aimlessly began to dissect the backs of the heads of the boys seated in front of me. One had two ears that stuck straight out, and I thought, *Oh, my, that's ugly.* I was sure I would never marry a man who didn't have nice ears. That was twenty years before I met Tom Ream. Tom, by anyone's standards, would pass as handsome, I think. Tom is angered when Ann and I describe him as handsome. That's not important to him. Let me add, he's much more than that. He's highly educated, a great father, and an ambitious, exciting man to live with. When I met him, he was a golden, bronzed tan with nicely styled hair below his ears and he looked delicious!

We fell in love and married. I never even thought of his ears until he got a businessman's haircut for an interview before leaving graduate school. I stood dumfounded when he walked out of the barber shop. I noticed for the first time (I had been married to him for six months) that one of his ears sticks out some. I couldn't believe this. I found myself wanting to take my hand and push it back flat and "make it right." I was traumatized by every haircut in those days, begging him to keep his hair long enough to camouflage his ear. His response, "Jan, no one ever in all my growing up years ever made fun of my ears." As each baby was delivered, my first concerns were their skin and ears. Our third son, born seven months ago, has gorgeous olive skin, dark hair, beautiful eyes with long dark eyelashes, but his ears aren't as flat as I'd like. Bless his heart. I headed for the store and found some tape and began taping them flat every night. What if the world would not find him beautiful? Sadly, I have had to struggle to shed this society's perspective that equates valuable and good with beauty.

Why has adult life handed me back a second time things I found almost too painful the first time around? I'm almost amused as I read this back to myself. We certainly do want life to hand back again the positive experiences to us, don't we? Am I looking for a perfect, flawless adult life? Free from what I lived and felt so much of as a child?

A brilliant, lovely client of mine years ago once shared with me that she married five months before their first daughter was born. She married only to give her child a father and give some resolve to this chaotic situation. Her second child, a daughter, was conceived at a terrible time in her life. She didn't want the baby and now had two children whose pregnancies had been disastrous emotional experiences. And while she had grown to love these children dearly, they had come into this world unwanted. She conceived her third child out of desire to do so and did everything imaginably "right" for a pregnant woman to do. This child was going to be her perfect child. She would make up for all she had failed to do the first two times. When the baby was born, a son, he had a serious kidney defect and died ten days later. She was going to bury her pain and failure and cover the wound with success. Instead she was handed her imperfection back again. Why?

It is our pain that offers us hope for more purity and wholeness. The more I look at it and study it, the more strongly convinced I am that it is our painful experiences that take us by the shoulders and bring us into a much clearer understanding of how human and finite we really are. It is our pain that leads us back to the places in ourselves that are still crippled. Pain reveals to us the parts of ourselves that aren't whole yet. We throw temper tantrums about this. We don't want to be imperfect. We want to be little gods with no need of help and no flaws. And because we don't want to accept these disfigured places in us, we cannot accept them in others. We develop bigotry toward these areas in others' lives and project onto them what we can't accept in ourselves. The people who cause us the greatest discomfort and who we are the most critical of are those people who are most like us. Until we wrap our arms around our failures, weaknesses, and imperfections, we will repel away from ourselves people with similar weaknesses. We'll then fail to find our way to those issues in life that are the most important issues, far greater than those we are focusing on. God and life seem to bring us back to re-experience our pain and give us an opportunity to deeper purity and wholeness—to teach us profound truths we missed the first time around. We are offered again the privilege to open our arms to all other humans as weak and imperfect as we are. What have you really learned from your pain? If I have been handicapped by a car accident somewhere, I must deal with my crippled condition until I can open my arms to all others who are crippled and no longer view it as a pitiful tragedy but rather as a rare opportunity.

If I have grappled with feelings of physical defectiveness, then I must deal deeply enough to realize how temporary and insignificant beauty really is to a meaningful and significant life.

Saturday night I had flown in from a speaking trip in Dallas, Texas, with a dynamic group of women. I was exhausted but content. Sunday we joined some friends for dinner. The husband of the young couple whom I shall call Joe began talking about a fabulous interview he had arranged for his wife. "She really impressed him," he said. "The man said he has great ideas and plans for her." Suddenly I felt a stab of pain. A pain I've come to recognize quickly. All of my childhood years were racked with messages and feelings of insignificance. The most frightening fear of my adult life has been that I will return to being that insignificant person again. I have put more energy into fighting that from happening probably than toward anything else I've tackled. My senses were blurred from the moment he announced his wife's future greatness. I gummed down my food, put most of my attention on Christian, my baby, and was ready to leave long before we did.

Once home, I put the baby in his crib and the phone rang. A friend, a dynamic, warm, brilliant woman who is also a physician called to tell me of an offer and her acceptance of a "position of a lifetime," and that she and her husband would be moving in a few months. I almost envied the thrill of that moment for her. I relish those moments when I, too, have experienced success. (Well, I was becoming more insignificant by the moment.) I hung up and began to pray. "God, teach me something about this pain. I'm in emotional agony." A series of thoughts began to run through my consciousness as God seemed to teach me Himself, something I had been too blinded to see.

Joe, my friend's husband, has a high-powered job and a lavish executive office he takes everyone who comes to town to see. His life is full of trappings—luxury cars, furs, expensive watches, and the latest gadgets. He always seems to present his trappings to the world and most of us fall short. Tom and I defi-

nitely do. And the picture I began to see was that his posses-
sions are his way of dealing with pain—his pain deep down,
probably from childhood, that he wasn't good enough—of inferiority. He takes care of that pain by making sure he stacks up
more trappings than the rest of us. If I buy a Gucci watch, he
buys a Cartier for his wife. I never have come away from him
feeling that I was "as good as" he is. I suddenly realized why I
had always had so much trouble with him, and why I had felt
pain with his wife's future success. It's because he reinforced in
me what I had felt for years. I wasn't *as good as.* I got a glimpse of
how deep his pain must be, and I found my heart brimming with
compassion and love for him. He suffers too. Underneath I've
only longed for his approval and lived half-angry because I
didn't feel I had it. In that moment my deeper understanding of
his needs transcended my need to be approved. I really do want
his wife's success. She only wants to live significantly and mean-
ingfully like I do.

The next picture was one of my clients with a vora-
cious appetite, who eats two weeks worth of groceries in two
days and throws it up, and I realized she tries to bury her screaming pain with food. That's her approach to her pain.

And then I saw myself. Striving and expending great
efforts to make sure I stay somewhat significant in this world. If
it means taking an extra client and being overbooked so I can
claim success, I do it. My memory suddenly recalled the words
of a father who had brought his daughter to me.

"I have gone to the same church with you every Sunday for two years and you haven't as much as spoken one word to
me, and now you want me to open up and tell you my heart? I
can't!" Those words challenged my life. You see, I hadn't tried
to ignore him. I like this man. It's just that I'm too busy taking
care of my own pain. Worrying as I walk into church if I'm still
loved and holding my own? I've been so busy taking care of *my*
pain I was missing the world around me. I was missing the greatest, most significant purpose of life for a man or woman, and
that is to take care of ourselves the best we can, find and love
God with all our hearts, souls, and minds as the Bible teaches,
and reach out and help those around us make it through.

I was suddenly repulsed by my own behavior. The

selfishness and self-centeredness I saw. What I had been trying to do was legitimately just take care of my pain—real, hurting, searing pain. So were the other two people I had seen in my thinking that day. None of us is trying to hurt anyone, just soothe our wounds. But how tragic. How much we are all missing. Regardless of how many standing ovations I've received and how many people I can say I've seen as a therapist...regardless of the "alumna of the year" award I had just received, nothing has ever been enough to free me from my pain nor to allow me to see you as clearly as I needed to.

In that moment I didn't want to be better than anyone. I yearned for no more badges of success. I just began to want more than anything else in this world to crawl down off my pedestal and join all the rest of hurting humanity at the foot of the cross. I saw that only knowing God and connecting with you, and *together*—and three of us making it—really matters. It gave me a new vision for life—new prescription for treatment of my "insignificant" obsession.

I enjoy speaking, and the affirmation of people and those great moments when I feel the world stamps me as *successful*—the thrill of being able to pen my convictions. But these aren't where my heart is anymore. I want to be a healer, not a heroine. I want to join you and take your hand and walk through life—just the days and weeks and months of experiences life will bring you and me and know at the end of life I have truly lived.

# ann

wholeness does not mean an absence of pain. it does not equate with perfection. rather it is just the opposite. struggle with flaws & pain are very essential to fulfillment.

the first real physical pain i remember was as a very small girl. running down a country road near a farmhouse where my parents were visiting, i had my arms spread on either side to feel the wind & sun & momentum better. a wasp was merrily flying along, right in the path of my open hand, & gave me an awful sting. it was such an abrupt, terrible surprise at a moment when i was experiencing such delight, that from then to now i have hated, & been fearful of, stinging insects, & i learned to run with my arms down.

then there was the time, on new skates, i decided to try this rather steep decline at the end of our street, & went flying, face downward, on the pavement. does *anything* sting much more than a pavement burn? i learned to be more cautious on hills.

there have been ear infections & stomach flu & diarrhea & menstrual cramps & appendicitis. in the last three years, the nine hospitalizations with miscarriage, life-threatening infections, surgeries to try to help conception.

but for the most part, i have been one of those exceptionally healthy people. rarely sick. strong. but for everyone, there are moments of physical discomfort. aspirin or bed rest usually resolves that, in time.

the pain of inferiority…of the fear of failure…of uncertainty…of rejection…of embarrassment…of failure itself—

that is a different level & dimension of pain that can be quieted & healed only by process—time—earnest effort.

growing up, my greatest pain was that i was a minority. an outsider in hawaii. a "haole." everyone was dark, i was fair. everyone was buddhist or hindu. i was Christian. my father was a preacher, nonetheless. most everyone was petite. i was tall. i stuck out.

it was very subtle, the rejection i felt. the kids collecting at lunchtime & recess in little cliques. my white face standing at the side of the building, watching. lonely. embarrassed. the japanese twins who were in our same class. their beautiful skin. the exquisite clothes they wore to school every day. their shiny, black hair. not even my twinhood amounted to much when you put those two girls next to us.

once, when i was in sixth grade, we were to learn the gettysburg address & repeat it, by memory, in front of the class. for some reason, i felt i could not do that. the thought of standing before my dark peers in my white skin & stringy pony tail was overwhelming to me. when the teacher called my name, i burst into tears & said, "i can't"—to that point, i had been an honor student. was in one of the brightest classes. the teacher took my response seriously & gave me a few days. to this moment, i remember the terror i felt doing that assignment.

of course, the phys. ed. classes where we had to dress down to shorts or swimsuits, & my not wanting anyone to see what i thought was a white, skinny, ugly body. teams being chosen, & my being one of the last selected for a team. never hitting the ball when my team needed *anything* to help them. college days when other girls seemed to have too many more exciting dates. when other girls were being elected to the homecoming court, & class offices, & i was struggling & silently begging the world to reassure me that i was special. the morning i was almost fired from my cafeteria job because i stumbled over a dish stack, & broke all 30 juice glasses i was carrying on a tray.

i remember wishing i could pick up algebra as fast as that one kid. that my handwriting was as pretty as another girl's. that i could play the piano as well as pam, the girl several years younger than i at church. they all seemed to receive so much recognition for these feats. such affirmation. i longed for praise. to feel special & valued.

church camp every summer. that always brought out a unique pain in me. jan & i washed & starched every dress we owned, & hauled most of our wardrobe to the cabin bunkhouse. trying to feel pretty. as good as everyone else. to measure up. there were always great moments at camp, but as the week went by, certain kids always rose to the top. were the leaders. the captains of the teams. girls began pairing off with boys. i felt an insatiable desire to belong in that group. popular. respected. attractive & exciting to the boys. looked up to.

i wish today i knew what happened to all the "most popular" kids in high school & college. have they all turned out to be spectacular successes? to be totally adjusted, & world changers? to be the upper crust of society? i do not remember hearing any of their names. watching them on television. reading their scientific journals. did all those popular, beautiful girls get the best men? yes, i wish i knew what happened to everyone who seemed to have such an edge on me & others in all my growing-up years!

i did not get elected to songleader, & the taste of defeat was brutal, but i learned to go on. to push beyond defeat, & just in the pushing & the surviving, i grew stronger. it probably did more for my internal character than victory ever could have.

there was no way i could, overall, change my skin tone or my crooked toes or banish every single freckle. or make myself a genius in math or an athletic superhero. i did learn to compensate. to be conscious of my clothes & well groomed. to smile a lot so people would notice my straight, white teeth. to develop my gifts in forensic speech & creative writing class & the school plays. i will never be good in softball, but i can play decent tennis, & i have learned to run a smooth, gliding, 7–7½ minute pace in long-distance races.

because jan & i did not receive a lot of applause & swarms of people wanting to attach to us, we did learn to *really* appreciate *every* kindness any human being ever directed our way. we try *never* to take for granted a compliment, a small gesture of love, a handclasp, a look that says, "i value you." we absorb every human extension to us, & enjoy it. to feel grateful.

wanting a baby since i was a small girl & not even marrying until 35, & not getting a baby for three years after that made me appreciate the gift so much more. the pain of patience is profound & wrenching.

the pain of waiting. for years. longing for something close by & yet so far from one's reach. begging & pleading to God. trying to help God when He seems slow. seeking others' help. others' prayers. looking for shortcuts. trying every avenue. one wall after another. one crashing blow, & another one before you can hardly get back on your feet from the last one.

i know this pain exists in singles wanting to find a really significant, meaningful relationship. to marry & have a home. have the security of that intimacy & seeming safety.

the pain lives in many trying to find social & financial success. to make it to the top. to gain recognition & prestige in one's job. for a man, his career, i think, is as vital to his well-being as his marriage. "honey, which do you love more—potatoes or me?" i ask will often, laughing. he loves potatoes. shipping them to iraq or sweden or florida. growing them. packing them. eating them. he replies, "to make a man choose between his wife & his life's work is like cutting off one of his legs. they are both so essential to his peace & joy."

for me, the pain was not being able to conceive a child, & then, when i did, miscarrying. it was month after month of hoping, trying, praying. of trying to be a perfect person (impossible) so God would not punish me & withhold this dream i clung to more than all others. every month my period would come, & the anguish. the tears. the feeling of defectiveness.

i would try to imagine what it would be like to be pregnant. the joy, the ecstasy. what it was like when i was, way back when. i would fantasize. when our baby, taylor, was born, i was with his mother through labor. 18 hours. i would run into the hall for moments & cry. somehow i wanted *me* to be delivering this baby. it would make me feel so much more whole & complete. though i was not the birth mother, it was one of the most magnificent moments of my life. there was the pain & sorrow of so wanting to experience pregnancy & delivery, but the blessing of walking out of the hospital—will & i & 1½ day old taylor—without stitches & twenty extra pounds to lose & leaking breasts…was wonderful.

out of the unique & choking sorrow of infertility has come in me the birth of such compassion of tenderness for *anyone* around me who is suffering. especially those who long for something they cannot seem to get.

the ten million couples who are pleading for babies to adopt. the one in five couples who are infertile, yet trying. all the women who, even today, received negative pregnancy tests, & are crying somewhere in dark bedrooms. the men & women standing in bars after work & going to the spa, trying to find a meaningful, deep relationship. the mother who has lost her son. the wife who longs for a nice home. the man who tirelessly tries to make it & never can seem to hit the big time.

prayerfully, i will never blurt out the news now that i am pregnant, & seemingly healthily so, to a woman who aches from an empty womb. i will never, without thinking, boast of my next book to be published to some fledgling writer who tastes getting even a poem or 1500 word essay into a magazine. i will try & not talk about how much i can eat without gaining weight.

no, there cannot be wholeness without pain. if i never again felt lonely or sad, i would lose touch with all of you who do. if i never failed, i could not grasp the glory of success. if i had never run an awful, hot, grueling marathon, i never would have appreciated those when i just seemed to fly along, & came to the finish line actually exhilarated.

if will & i never misunderstood each other, i would not have learned the peace & joy i feel on the days when we are truly connecting & growing as a team.

if my baby never cried, i would not feel, so deeply, the magic of his laughing eyes.

if i had not been single 35 years, i might not be aware of your longing to hold or be held. to be intimate. to build dreams together. i have longed for those things for years, & when God brought the gift of will, i appreciated everything so much more.

pain is one of my best friends. it teaches me as nothing

else can. it reminds me who i am not, & who you are. it leads me to God.

pain is bringing me to my purest self. to a love & sensitivity & feeling for others that goes far beyond sympathy & casual condolence. pain is teaching me to laugh with you & cry with you & stick with you over all the lonely roads. it has taken the accumulation of years & years of normal, growing up pain to find the real values. the answers that make a difference. the courage to rise above defeat. the strength to face a mountain & conquer it & watch it crumble. to move beyond to the next one.

& all our pain has led jan & me to you. to say we care. in some way, we understand. we run beside you. we love you. you are not alone.

no matter how dark your road today, or how long & seemingly endless your tunnel, you will laugh again. the sun will shine. pain will lead you out to a whole, new, wide, brilliant place.

# 12.

# *Friendship*

## ann

jan always had so many friends. i was more reserved & cautious in opening myself to others. much more afraid of letting anyone get too close to me. in the last ten years, it has been very easy to speak to thousands from a stage. on some levels, i could be very intimate with the crowds, but they were "down there" i was up, away from them. i would fly out the next morning & no one could get closer than i wanted them to.

jan has taught me that real friendships are vital to my well-being. when i married in boston, & moved to idaho with will, it was the first time in years that i had to live a so-called normal life. to face the same people day in & day out. to see the same faces every sunday at church. i was not breezing in & out every week (after marriage, i cut way back on my speaking engagements). most of the women around me were young mothers.

often, on very lonely days, i would try to think of *anyone* i could call locally & just talk to. though i knew anyone would probably be open to my connecting, i never had the courage to reveal anything about myself to anyone. yes, at that point i had written eight books...best-sellers...traveled the world ...spoken to big crowds—but i was terrified of intimacy. of people finding out who i *really* was underneath all the success. just an everyday, struggling, *very* human person. afraid that by peeling back the mystique of accomplishment, & showing the *real* me, i would lose their respect & warmth & admiration & love.

my best friend in the world was jan. when one has an identical twin sister who has shared all of life with her, it is easy to just cling to that relationship, & move away from others. i married, & became friends with will. there was a part of me, at that point, that hid behind him. with will & jan, i found myself saying, "that is enough."

117

but i was so lonely. so longing to laugh & chat with…commiserate with & unveil to…other people.

one of the greatest gifts in life is friendship. people coming together & establishing real trust & vulnerability & love. fishing & boating & running together. eating popcorn & ice cream together. talking over dinner with plates pushed back & elbows pressed down. people dreaming together. sharing secrets. wounds. fears. pulling off masks. God may not allow us all to be financially rich. to drive expensive cars & live in sprawling houses. to have notoriety & prestige. but these gifts are not essential to joy & beauty, laughter, & fun. to feeling secure & whole. to knowing you can make it through any crisis.

it's people coming together. sharing on the deepest levels. there is nothing richer.

my father was a preacher. when jan & i were 3 & 4 years old, he pastored in houston, texas. an old lady, with wisps of gray hair flying everywhere, was our baby-sitter & friend, mrs. thrash. she made us feel we were the most fabulous children on earth. she told us stories. had little surprises. got down on the floor & played dolls with us. hid in closets for us to find. she instilled such self-worth in us even as four-year-olds. her house was old. very ordinary. she was over 80, wrinkled, faded dresses. from the outside, we would have viewed her as having common life experiences. but not so. her world danced with merriment & magic & surprise.

another couple, friends of my parents, were percy & marie. she had beautiful figurines on her tables, & brocade bedspreads, air conditioning. percy always made hot biscuits for breakfast. marie was always pulling some elegant dress out of the closet & giving it to my mother. they treated jan & me as if we were as valuable as my parents. called me "sweetie." teased us in a fun-loving way.

mrs. sanders, a white-haired nurse, for years sent us surprises in the mail. new little store-bought dresses, handkerchiefs, $10 now & then. when we would visit her where she lived, she would always treat us to dinner at some elegant, gracious restaurant.

one night, sitting in a grand, large room with white-linen tablecloths & napkins & smartly dressed waiters, jan whispered, "daddy, is this the *public?*"

we had been taught to always behave our best in "public." whatever exactly that meant we were not sure.

the wylies were in texas. they had thousands of acres of land. talked with a southern drawl. lived in an old house outside dallas where they had all grown up. there was always homemade pecan pie & big, juicy steaks even for us as children. my mother could play the old grand piano in the living room, & we would sit around & sing with her. stories were swapped & shared. elva ruth wylie always took us to neiman's tearoom for lunch. gorgeous models were everywhere, displaying the latest fashions. the food was exquisite, the service impeccable.

as a child, those family friendships changed my life. they created memories for me that nothing else could have. memories of feeling close & valued & loved & enjoyed & cherished.

for years, after i became an adult, i would spend hours with children, trying to put into them what friendship had put into me at their ages. often, i took a child, usually from a poorer neighborhood, on my trips to speak. an airplane experience. pizza & ice cream & hugs & surprises for a day or two. today, i let neighbor girls bring sleeping bags to our living room. fix them *whatever* they like to eat. always keep treats around if they stop by. talk about their hair & new boots & dolls. a beautiful, small boy down the street wants to grow up & be a writer. he puts little stories in my mailbox. i read them & critique them & put them back in his mailbox, usually with a surprise cookie or piece of candy.

rolfe & dot, in baton rouge, with grown children & grandchildren, pick me up at the airport (and now, will, if he happens to be on that particular trip). they throw their arms around me. give me the prettiest room in the house. fix my favorite foods. with my friends, marie & nancy, in washington, d.c., we give each other facials, & talk about our new wrinkles, & attend some extravaganza in town. paul & margaret call from iowa just to say they love will & me.

once, before i married, i decided to take raymond & sally & their children with me to ski in vermont. raymond was an all-pro football player, but had never skied. we all piled into two adjoining rooms. we flew down hills. often, sally & i would

sit down & slide when the speed got too great & we were terrified of careening into a tree & perishing. our rears were constantly soaked & cold. we screamed & shrieked & followed each
other through the white wonderland. after hours, we would
stumble into the lodge, numb & frozen, & drink hot cider &
linger in front of the roaring fire. in the evening, we would
enhale exotic cuisine, ravenous & exhausted.

will creates so much fun in friendship. he brings people together. dresses us all in cumbersome, oversized snow suits,
rents snowmobiles, & takes us down seemingly forbidden, unknown paths through woods. he organizes fishing parties & ca-
noes & rafts on swelling rivers. once, when we had another
couple over, he found a bicycle for each of us. we biked miles, all
over town, & had a progressive dinner. stopping at all the favorite fast-food places, we would order one thing & have it divided
four ways. then we would bike on to the next place.

no one can take memories away. for you & for me,
there are bad memories & good ones. through friendships, one
can make enough good memories to completely overshadow the
bad ones. to keep merriment in one's mind. to keep one smiling
even on impossible days. to help us feel safe even when the alli-
gators are eating our toes & the world is pressing in.

health can go. loved ones can be taken, even suddenly.
jobs are lost. dreams are sometimes dashed. wars & earthquakes
can come. but beautiful memories around strong, faithful friendships are ours forever. we can draw on them & chew them in our
minds for years, & find value & joy.

sure. people fail. sometimes. friendships take a lot of
work, energy, patience, time. sometimes there is pain. sometimes honest moments that hurt. anything of value, though, requires a cost. a price to be paid. some loss. some gain.

reach out, as i am trying to do more & more in my little world in idaho. open yourself. nurture friendships. some
more intense than others. love. share. give. surprise a child with
a gift. have a neighbor or couple drop by for dessert. buy groceries for an invalid. take a tent & invite another couple along
& cook out under the wide sky!

hold a hand. pat a shoulder. kiss a tired cheek. make a
bowl of popcorn. call the world your friend. laugh & cry with
her. not too long ago we did just that.

it had been a hard day for will & me. a lot of reasons. in the evening, i pulled my heavy coat on over a flannel nightgown & knee socks. will picked up a baskin-robbins ice-cream cake, & we drove to friends, unexpectedly. our children played. we ate ice cream cake & talked about our struggles. we found time to laugh. then to pray. we headed home & the whole world looked better. & a piece of sunrise crept into our dark corner.

# Jan

Tom and I attended a surprise fortieth birthday party last week for a friend of mine, given by a woman who is a mutual friend of us both. She wanted to help Mary successfully begin this monumental crossing over from youth into maturity. I had been speaking in Michigan and arrived home with only time to wash my face and grab my gift off the counter unwrapped. Tom and I mutually agreed as we faced this group of people, most of whom neither of us knew, that this was not our kind of thing. Basically, we both felt somewhat shy. And to make it worse, I was coming into this elegant group of people with my gift, a beautiful cut-glass nightlight, not elegantly wrapped with an appropriate card but carrying it like I had bought it at the corner store as a last-minute thought. I tried not to berate myself too badly. In the midst of speaking, clients in crisis, and three children, it was the best I could do.

When we got to the front door of the house, we could hear loud music playing, laughter, and the sounds of many people into celebrating. I was too tired to celebrate. Tom and I both, born into homes of evangelical ministers, were more accustomed to church parties. But I deeply love these two women and was not going to miss cheering my friend on into this new era in her life for any reason. When I rang the bell, the music was so loud no one heard, and finally I pushed open the door myself, and we entered a charmingly decorated century-old home, full of balloons and strangers. When my one friend (the hostess) saw me, she hurried across the room and threw her arms around me. I introduced Tom and handed her my unwrapped gift and muttered something about my plane being late and could she find some wrapping paper? With not even a hint of disapproval she enthusiastically took my gift and left to pour us some Diet 7-up. Tom and I headed for the room filled with people. They were an electrifying group. The women and men smartly dressed, interacting vivaciously with each other. As soon as my friend for whom the party was being given saw us from the other side of the room, she shrieked ecstatically toward me. She couldn't believe I had come. In that moment I wasn't sure who was the honored guest, she or I! My feelings of insignificance and shyness slipped down around my ankles as she embraced Tom and me and began introducing us to this roomful of attractive people. I knew at that moment this was going to be a great evening. I was loved. Not because I was the most beautiful or carried the most impressive credentials, but simply for some intrinsic quality. Suddenly, I felt free to be me and began to lose myself in discovering the beauty and magic of the interesting people around me. It was an evening full of elegance, laughter, celebration, scrumptious food, and love. I went to give love but found transformation in the love I received.

Great friendships are essential to healthiness and wholeness. Friendship is one of the most significant ways we experience ourselves.

When someone laughs at our jokes:

- or sits enrapt as we tell a story
- or lets tears surface and spill over as we share a sorrow
- or allows us to touch their hands and create smiles on their faces

we are able to know beyond any doubt we are not just a blob of invisible gas. We are a real flesh-and-blood-human being. We can arouse an emotion or reaction out of another human. Our existence can be confirmed.

It is always interesting, I think, to ask ourselves what are the qualities we look for in our deep friendships. We are all different, so what you look for may be different from what I look for. I have a great respect and love for all humanity and find nearly all people interesting and enjoyable. Yet the people I desire to be with the most are those who are affirming. They translate to me in some way, "You are a valuable person." They are willing to be vulnerable, to take my hand, and in comradship say, "I have pain, too." And I think they are people who enjoy some of the things I enjoy. Research shows that the happiest married couples are those who enjoy a lot of common interests. I guess I'm saying we choose deep friendships of people who help us meet what we need to survive in this world. A good friend of ours Reuben Welch wrote a book *We Really Do Need Each Other.* What a great plan of God!

One day I looked directly into the eyes of a man who had raised a marvelous daughter and asked, "How did you do it? What was your secret?" He replied, "We didn't do it alone. We had great friends. She went to good schools. We belonged to a spiritual and supportive church. We didn't raise her alone." We need, as the great psychiatrist William Glasser says, "People who love us and people we can love back."

This is not to say friendship is easy. To commit oneself to a relationship and to working out the differences is a huge undertaking.

Over the years I've had some clients who found it difficult to make and keep friends. More than once after a fifty-minute session with them I could understand why. However, regardless of how tough it might get for both of us, I will be there the next week to keep working out the conflicts. For some they feel they have to pay to find that kind of relationship.

There are moments I can't stand myself, and it's no wonder others have trouble with me. God bless the people who hang in with me through my awful, disgusting moments. I've heard Tom say to our children. "You can't do anything to make me stop loving you. Whatever happens in life, your mother and I are here to stand behind you."

A deeply committed missionary couple shared with me that their fourteen-year-old son began to rebel on the mission field of the foreign land they were serving in. Rather than lecture the child on how bad he was, they sat him down and said, "We know this is a very difficult time for you. We want you to know if and when it gets too much for you to handle just let us know, and we will gladly pack up and move back to the States. You mean more to us than anything else."

We need people who will not just be there for laughter and good times but who will put an arm around our shoulder, and believe in us when we can't believe in ourselves—who will agree from the beginning of the relationship that there will be conflicts between us, but we will struggle until we have worked them out.

One night I was confronting Tom with some issue in our marriage that was bothering me. He sat and stared blankly. My earnest cry for help was being met by a lack of reciprocity. Finally, I burst into tears and sat down with an "I give up" sign. Tom looked at me and said, "Jan, I know I'm having difficulty understanding but just keep going. Let's not give up." Well, that sounded logical. I did and eventually we connected.

It was 2:00 A.M. Tre, seven years old, had fallen off the top bunk bed. I pulled him in bed with Tom and me and for the next forty-five minutes he tossed and squirmed. The baby woke and Tom tumbled out of bed to check, and I wondered if maybe we should just all get up and get some work done. I knew Tre was going to awaken exhausted for school, and I had an eleven-hour-client load ahead of me.

I said, "Tre, you're having trouble sleeping, aren't you? What are you thinking about?" "John." His teacher, a very energetic and high-strung man, out to produce Rhodes scholars. I wanted to say, "Now, honey, he's a wonderful man who tries very hard to get you to reach your potential." My therapeutic self triggered in, however, and responded with, "Tell me what you're feeling, honey." "I would just like to tell John I'd like him to compliment my work more often." "Tre, that would be a great thing to say. Tell him, dear," I responded. "He might get mad," Tre quickly retorted. "What would you say then?" I confronted. "Well, I could say 'I feel bad when you get angry.'" "Excellent, Tre. You could." "Mommy, why don't you be John, and I'll be Tre, and let's see how I do." At 2:45 A.M. we role-played and talked about assertiveness. The importance of using *I* statements and expressing what it is *I* am feeling in an appropriate way. I saw that night that John was in Tre's life for a purpose. Tre needs to learn to face someone who is strong and still maintain his own personhood. At 3:00 A.M. I hugged my wonderful, magical, little son and said, "Honey, it's been wonderful talking to you tonight." And he squeezed my neck and rolled over and fell sound asleep. He needed someone to "hear" his heart. To accept what he was feeling as valid. To affirm to him he wasn't all bad. It was as if God had stopped the crazy busyness of my life and carved out a piece of quiet so I could connect to my own seven-year-old son in friendship and help him make it through the night. That's why I need you and you need me.

# 13.

# Conflicts

## ann

when i was dean of women on a college campus back east, i was almost as young as some of the girls. the job had been offered to me when i was four years out of college myself, & though i felt i could learn to handle it, i had very little life experience under my belt.

a dean oversees all the girls, the staff, the dormitories. it is definitely a people-related position. conflicts are a part of every day's agenda.

one particular couple, brilliant, both professors, had a daughter on campus. at one point, i had to move her room. there were some other i-thought-minor situations, but slowly i began to hear whisperings of criticism toward me as the dean. the parents did not come to me face-to-face, but the stinging pieces of negatives that continually floated into my office wiped me out.

one day, we all met in my office. it was time for us to confront each other. to make our statements not to others but to the ones involved. out of that honest sharing came understanding & resolve & respect.

much harder for me than writing a book or making a speech or doing the laundry is trying to work through conflicts.

one young woman regularly wrote me eight-to-ten-page single-spaced letters about her frustration with & disdain of me. her anger that my life seemed so perfect. that God must love me more. that it was not fair. her criticism of my writings, of my not responding often enough to her mail. her fury when i got married & left her single. she was gifted in subtlety, tearing me apart. making me feel guilty for ever being happy. for ever trying to do anything good. for even finding a husband. i would read these pages, week after week, & be stripped of joy. angry myself at such put-downs.

i tried everything to resolve this conflict. sent her loving notes, asking forgiveness for any way i failed her. telling her i loved her. i cared. i did several favors for her that she had asked of me. i prayed for her. she twisted every note. she blasted me for mentioning something will & i had done, saying i was insensitive to where she was.

finally, after trying every idea possible, it came to me that i must not let her do this to me. it was distorted. harmful. she was probably enjoying manipulating my feelings, & making me feel awful & guilty. so i stopped not only answering her letters. i now do not even read them.

what a sad way to end a conflict. some people do not let you do it any other way. they leave you no options. with some, there is no peace. no happiness. no resolve. you lay the burden down & move on, knowing it is not your problem to solve.

there can be conflict even with children. one little girl in my neighborhood began coming to my front door sometimes several times a day. often ringing the doorbell when the baby was sleeping, & i was. will might tell her not to come for a couple of days because i would be busy, but she would call anyway & ask me if she could come.

"honey, whatever will says, goes. you need not call me after he has already told you what he wants for the next couple days."

this child comes from a lovely home. a really thoughtful, wise, good mother. but she was pushy. she found a way to get what she wanted.

will & i talked about it. should i discuss this with her mother? i really didn't want to because i would not want to offend her for any reason. i loved the family. i loved this child. i just did not like her running our lives for us.

one day she called. "ashley, i would like you to come over so we can talk."

when she knocked on the front door, there she stood with her school friend. "i brought mary over to meet you & play with little taylor, too." pretty smart for a child! she did not want confrontation. she knew, instinctively, that her pushy behavior was getting to me, but she had outsmarted me again.

next, i just waited for her to come over alone. sitting down beside her on the couch, i said, "ashley, real friendship is not crowding anyone. it is not pushing people around. bossing everyone. making them fill your needs. our being friends means you respect me...my privacy, my home, my husband & baby. you come over only after first calling & checking it out. you do not call after talking to will, hoping i will give you another answer...

"you are young. people will not like you if you do not change. people are not to be manipulated. used. if you do not change your behavior, you will not have any friends as you grow up. that will really make me sad. i love you. i see great potential in you. let's work on this."

it is amazing how teachable children can be if they know you really care. really love them. if someone sees my child off the track, & can lovingly steer him back on, it will mean so much to me. confrontation takes so much more energy than living with the situation. than overlooking everything. but there is no growth without it, & eventually, something disintegrates in the relationship.

one friend of mine has really loved me. she will run any errand for me. take me anywhere. try to find a solution to my problem i cannot seem to resolve. surprise me with ice cream or a piece of candy. send me a beautiful card in the mail. i know she is utterly loyal, & her heart is right.

somehow, this kind of relationship can become too close. she started dressing just as i did. if i walked 10 miles, she went out & walked 15. i began to feel overwhelmed. competitive. threatened. will would remind me what a compliment it is to have someone copy you. i understood that, yet rather than feeling refreshed by it, i began to resent this person. to lose a sense of who i was. to feel she would become better than i. then she would no longer need me to look up to. to admire. she would fly on down the road & leave me.

she did things for me because i *know* she really loved me. but it also gave her a sense of control over my life. i so wanted to be accepted by her that i let her control so many of the details. in the process, i lost a handle on my own life that i had always had. it stripped me of some basic self-esteem & confidence that was essential to my wholeness.

it took a lot of work on both our parts to develop a healthy relationship. a lot of honesty. she, more & more, began to find her own style of dress. i confessed my insecurity concerning her becoming better than i someday. she told me she walked farther than i did to try to impress me & make me think she was more valuable.

in time, i became more assertive, more detached. i had to go back to doing some of the tasks she had taken over for me so i could feel more in control of my own world. oh, the work of coming to peace with each other. of getting very close. of seeing one as he/she truly is. the flaws. the foibles of still loving & accepting each other.

of sometimes crying & screaming over the phone. of asking forgiveness. of picking up & going on to a new place. of sometimes building space. of knowing too much closeness can destroy the intimacy. of learning to laugh. to wear even the heavy moments as lightly as possible. to have a short memory on hurting words spoken in anger & pain.

in marriage, conflicts are inevitable. for days, will & i can be in such harmony. loving. kind. gentle. suddenly, something erupts. one thing sets will off, & then he reacts & sets me off. & instantly all the peace & warmth is now a volcanic explosion.

for will & me, it is giving each other some space to cool off so we can rationally talk about it. my tendency, being so verbal, is to say hurtful, mean words, & i am *diligently* working at controlling my tongue. one's ability to control the tongue shows one's self-control. one's true strength. that only as you can keep hold on what comes out of your mouth can you really be whole.

will is constantly working at responding, & not reacting. often, with tears streaming down my face, i blurt out something unkind, & he will reach out & wrap his arms around me & hold me. for the most part, that's what i need. forgiveness. reassurance. not to feel rejected. a coming together. God must receive hours of humorous entertainment as He watches us down here. fighting over the silliest things. the most inconsequential issues.

there will always be conflict among us because we are human. sometimes threatened. other times scared & feeling put down or unsure. we are crippled in places & cannot always see things as they really are. we are physical, with hormonal changes. with sleepless nights & headaches.

wholeness comes out of conflicts. out of learning to work through them. face them. understand them. live with them. grow from them. wholeness says i am not afraid of conflicts. i will not let them destroy me or my love for you. i will let the conflict lead me to a truer place in you, & you in me.

# Jan

We were on our way home from Sunday church. Tom and Nash were in the front seat; Tre, Christian, and myself were in the back. We climbed into the car in front of the church and, as we did, we smiled and hugged our friends. I was effusive—the picture of confidence and joy—someone who felt thrilled to be alive. To those standing around, I'm sure I gave the air of having all I needed to make me happy. I am amazed sometimes at how skilled I am at painting a picture of success over underlying feelings of anxiety and low-grade depression.

This was also Tom's and my thirteenth wedding anniversary. For years we have notoriously gotten into an uproarious argument the day of our anniversary.

Suddenly, Tre, who was sitting next to me, threw his pen on the floor. He had stuck it unconsciously into his mouth full of bubble gum. The gum had stuck all over the top of this new pen he had just received as an award that morning. Try as he did, he could not get the bubble gum off.

He then began to focus on his Pac Man watch, which for some unknown reason began to defect and not work properly. He began to slap at the face of the watch and call it dumb. There was no question about it—the tension was mounting.

We were on our way to meet some friends at their new home for lunch and then we were all going to head for a parade close by.

Tom called back for a Granola Bar, and Tre threw one forward. This seemed to me to be a displacement of Tre's frustration, but it definitely irritated Tom. Tom told Tre sternly he was not to throw things in the car. Then Tre burst into tears and retorted, "Well, if I'm not to throw things in the car, how come you threw that hard-boiled egg into the front seat on that trip we took to Pennsylvania?" By this point he was sobbing.

Tom refused to respond. He rigidly continued to drive in the direction of our friends' home. Tre was crying quietly, and I angrily sat waiting for Tom to give an answer, at least, to Tre's statement. After about twenty seconds, it was obvious Tom was not going to answer Tre, whom he perceived to be totally out of place. I finally exploded, "Answer him, Tom. He at least deserves that!" Tom icily told me to "shut up" or we would end up back home. I hate being put in corners or given ultimatums. I screeched back, "I will not stop," and with that, Tom spun the car around and headed home. I began to scream, "We can't go home. These people are expecting us. We will ruin their afternoon." Tom coldly replied that he couldn't imagine our family doing anything but ruin their afternoon in the state we were in. I can't tell you how horrible it was. I think we all felt trapped, frustrated, and determined to hang on to our own positions. Nash and Christian were sitting wide-eyed observing the process.

When we got home, I flew out of the car, slamming the car door, and headed for the phone. "Susie, we are in a horrible state of conflict. I'm humiliated to even have to admit such. I realize we are due at your house this minute and, to be quite honest, I'm not sure there is any way we can pull out of this 'state of being' we're in, recover and still meet you."

Tom was waiting for me upstairs. I plopped into the nearest chair and said, "Honey, I'm sorry about all my ugliness, but I cannot stand the power position you take by refusing to talk. That is the ultimate power trip. Tre at least deserves an answer—a response."

"Jan, I honestly don't see any connection between the two incidents. I only see him trying to get out of his responsibility for his own actions."

At this point, Tre had wandered in and together we three began to talk out our feelings—Tre, crying behind a pillow he was holding over his face. Before the next fifteen minutes had passed, we had all apologized and had worked through to an understanding of where the other was coming from. I marched back to the phone and called Susie. "We will meet you at the parade. I think we've worked through our conflict."

Nash was begging us to hurry before we missed the whole parade. He had stayed in the car, entertaining Christian while Tom, Tre, and I had been talking through the issues.

As we started off once again, I began to pray out loud that God would somehow redeem this day that was originally planned to be fun and special. I told Tre and Nash that almost nothing can ruin a good day if we will just keep talking through our differences until we come to an agreement and mutual understanding. I am not sure Tre believed me.

There was a new peace—a quiet spirit in the car. I felt all of us began to put on our best behavior and attitudes to salvage this day. None of us wanted a disappointment—a failure—and we knew we each one would have to carry our own weight to keep things on an up note.

The parade was fun. We eventually met up with our friends and lived out a day that ended in closeness, forgiveness, understanding, and joy. On the way home that evening, Tre called from the backseat, "Mom and Dad, this really has turned into a good day!" There was a sweet, new camaraderie between Tre and Tom—a closer link between them than I have seen in a long time.

In therapy, I have said hundreds of times, I'm sure, "Conflict is not bad. It can always surface in meaningful relationships." The important issue is that there must be resolution. As horrid and acid and explosive as a scene can become between people who really do love each other, no permanent, deep harm will come if we can come back together, touch, be vulnerable, and give until we all have gained a new understanding of the dynamics going on. Everyone in the conflict must also feel his or her thoughts and feelings have been heard and understood. The real tragedy occurs when people have horrendous conflicts, which leave one or all of the individuals involved hurt, abused, and misunderstood. I say things I don't mean, and you do the same, but we never come back together and say, "We can't leave things in this state of fury and misunderstanding." We have to talk things out and keep talking and working until we can both (or all) come out feeling loved and valued by the others. The old adage "All is well that ends well" seems to hold a lot of truth.

In a conflict, it is important to remember that we all genuinely believe that what we feel and think is right. The only way a conflict is resolved is when we each one take the time to listen and begin to understand how the other person can see and feel the situation so differently.

We need to be committed to resolving our differences and to working them out. Security in the relationship comes when I know you will not abandon me if there is a conflict, a misunderstanding. You will not refuse to give as much time and energy as is needed until we are able to come back together with a warm, loving feeling between us. It is important for me to say that I find that *resolved conflicts* leave people in a deeper, tighter, more loving bond than they ever experienced with each other before. It cements more securely a love relationship.

Working through misunderstandings is the greatest source of our growing closer. If you have never had a conflict with a close friend or a family member, then one of you isn't exhibiting yourself. One or both of you are not being honest. Conflict is necessary for people to bond more strongly. It is not the conflict that brings us more intimately together but rather the working it through—the new insights and truths we begin to see in each other that, for some reason, we had not seen before. What two people have after working through a conflict is a closer relationship and with a new respect for each other.

I was in a Sunday church service one morning. It was a packed room—perhaps four hundred people present. The minister was expounding loudly on the importance of *never giving up*. He got off on a tangent at one point and began to talk about the fallacies of unions and work environments. It was pretty much a blue-collar congregation, and I am sure he began to arouse irritation in many of the parishioners listening. Suddenly, a striking six-foot-four-inch man two rows from the front stood to his feet, called the pastor by name, and firmly announced he felt the pastor was way out of line, and that he would be "walking out," which he proceeded to do. We were all stunned and aghast, none as strongly as the pastor himself. Taken by shock, he became defensive and asserted he was absolutely on target and proceeded to finish his sermon. How could he not when he was in the middle of a discourse on the importance of "never giving up!" Later that day, however, he drove to the man's house and apologized for offending him. The parishioner was not ready to budge or compromise on his difference of opinion.

To resolve a conflict, everyone has to be willing to work, to change, to surrender their "rightness." Resolution does not come from just one person saying, "I'm sorry," and the other walking away.

The next Sunday morning, that tall, handsome man again rose during the service, and a hush covered the room. I think we were all geared for another confrontation. "Pastor, I just want you and these people to know that I am sorry for the way I behaved last Sunday. I was wrong. We may not see eye-to-eye on that issue, but I was way out of place to stand and say the things I did." Wow! That is a sign of a workable person, someone capable of great intimacy, someone who determines to consider where I'm coming from, too. Again a sweet spirit filled that room.

If you really care deeply for me, and I for you, we will at some point run into a conflict. I hope we will persevere, talk and listen, until we cross the roaring river and reach a new level of depth, respect, and trust in each other. I am not afraid of conflicts. I am only afraid you will not address the conflict and work with me until we both find peace—peace with myself and peace with you. I want to get better at getting down to my true feelings, to what in me is being threatened. I need to learn to be more vulnerable, to say I'm sorry. Each one's feelings are so important.

Many people have years of hurt and anger stashed up and stored deep inside them from dozens of unresolved conflicts. I want to get close only to people who will be problem solvers. I know how imperfect a human I am. At some point in our relationship, I will most likely disappoint, offend, or differ from you. But we can work through our differences. We can walk miles and years together and contribute a lot of joy and meaning to each other's lives. If we cannot resolve our differences, a wall will be built between us and someday we will not have anything meaningful left between us.

# 14.
# Spirituality
## Jan

I was seven years old when I first heard the call of God. My parents had taken Ann and me to see a Billy Graham movie *Oil Town USA*. No one could ever convince me that a child cannot hear and respond to God's call because I did that night. Even then I think Ann took the first step and I followed. Ann, my greatest leader! That was the beginning of a long journey. I have known and walked with God for thirty-two years now.

The old-time evangelical church had a song, "Standing on the Promises of God." I've worked my way through life doing exactly that. Taking by faith the Bible teaching and that preached by my parents and stepping through my life watching the love and faithfulness of God lead me from darkness to light, from despair to hope, from selfishness to a greater concern for others, from insignificance to a much greater sense of who I am today than even I imagined earlier in my life. I have found no greater intimacy than that which God and I have established.

As a child, I would crawl beneath the covers and fall asleep quoting some great Scripture:

And we know that all things work together for good... (Rom. 8:28).

Trust in the LORD with all your heart...And He shall direct your path (Prov. 3:5,6).

And clinged tightly to the only hope for a child as simple and ordinary as I.

It came clearly to me several months ago, as I sat on the beach and watched my children play in the water beyond me, that God has wrapped up into each of us just exactly what we need to fulfill His perfect will for our lives. There are therapists far more brilliant than I, sitting in offices waiting for someone to help but He has given me the opportunity to help others. We were with a college president one evening, and he repeatedly would quote some current book and ask if I had read it. I would as graciously as possible respond "no." After presenting me with eight or ten books I had not read, I quipped sharply, "No, and if you ask me one more time about a book, I'm getting out of this car!" My husband saved the moment by adding "But she has read *I'm Out to Change the World* [one of Ann's books]," and we all laughed. I came home that night severely questioning God for not having made me smarter. Instead He gave me years of pain to carve an understanding heart and open doors of opportunity for me to walk into.

Tre and Nash and Christian are equipped with all the dimensions they need to fulfill their greatest potential. They must simply explore and develop what is inside and join God's great hand with friendship, salvation, and help and experience years of life.

If you could see where God has brought me *from* to where I am today then you would know the reason why I love Him so! I have traveled it seems like a million miles, many of them hard miles, to come to where I am today. I have struggled with a culture that didn't accept me, with a twin who has always kept me on my toes (and with whom I've had to resolve and determine what was unique in me), with a body that I would not have chosen. But today, looking back over my life, I can say, "It's been good."

I have a much clearer view of the world today. I used to only see a piece; now I see a broader picture. I'm sitting here at thirty-nine years old, penning my first words, after watching Ann publish nine best-sellers. And Ann is beside me carrying her first unborn child, after seeing me through three pregnancies.

I've heard so many times, "It was such a mistake to have married Bob"; or "I've made so many mistakes in raising my children." We've all made some grave mistakes—if we're honest with ourselves. It's part of being human. But mistakes can be our greatest teachers. Tom said to me once early in our marriage, "I always have believed that if I learn something from a mistake I've made then I cannot call it a failure."

I had always approached life from the perspective that I must be perfect. Mistakes were awful—evidence of failure and badness in my life. A few years ago, I began to stop beating myself up for each and every confirmation that I was not already an angel. I've learned to surrender my mistakes to God, confess them to you, and watch God use them in a creative way in my life. You and I must work at not focusing in on our failures, but rather on God's great power to take everything in our lives and turn it into good for us. We need to pile up all our mistakes into one big stack and lay them at the feet of God—for Peter who betrayed Jesus three times, and the woman caught in adultery, and Jonah who disobeyed. Over and over again, God has dared to believe in humanity in spite of our mistakes and failures and disobedience to His ways. Again and again He forgives and gives us another chance—another opportunity to try again—and uses everything—even our worst mistakes and failures to bring us something better.

I am assured that wherever you are today there is more for you to find and discover too. I don't care where you've come from. Or what sins you've committed. (I've committed many.) Or how many deadly mistakes you've made. My stack may be higher. Get back in the race. Start putting one foot down and then the other. Take the hand of God and let Him lead you.

# ann

the headlines of our local newspaper announced that a newborn male baby had been found in a dumpster, smothered to death. the body was still warm when a maintenance man found it.

shortly, thereafter, a young woman, with her boyfriend, were brought back from the east coast & charged with murder. everyone was enraged. people wanted to kill the young mother for what she did to an innocent baby.

"if i could get my hands on her...!"

several women i know in idaho falls, who are longing for a baby to adopt, were furious. they made statements full of such anger i was shocked. surprisingly, i did not feel as they did. yes, i had miscarried. yes, i had lost babies. yes, i longed for more babies. somehow, though, i felt compassion & pity & sadness for this young woman.

i made several speaking trips. was busy loving & mothering taylor. doing things with will. it had been several days since i had read the newspaper.

one afternoon, my secretary called me at home. someone from the jail had left a message. could i come see a young woman who was in serious trouble? the authorities were allowing her to visit with one clergy person. though she was from a mormon background, she chose to see me. one of the jailers loved my books & had been sharing them with her.

yes, of course i would come. leaving taylor with will, i pulled on a warm coat after dinner, & headed downtown.

cathy (not her real name) was lovely. clear, shining

blond hair. clear, pale skin. 20 years old. dressed in green khaki, the jail uniform. we were seated together in a private part of a corridor, at a small table. she was clutching tissues in her hand. washed gray walls. cold cement floors.

"cathy, tell me about you."

"well...i always liked school. i even usually made A's. until my dad committed suicide. he was my best friend. we were really close. he did it one day while i was home. it was awful, & suddenly i did not care anymore. i did not understand anything. my grades really dropped...but i went to night school, & got my high school diploma. my dream was always to be a teacher.

"about a year after my dad died, my brother was in a terrible car accident. it left him a paraplegic. i almost lost another very important person to me. it really upset me. i was not going to get close to any man again. i was not going to let anyone hurt me so much. then i met bob [not real name]. he was so kind. older. gentle. we have been together for 4 years. he was the father of the baby. he had been married once before. had to. & he kept saying he did not want any more kids like that.

"i think i blocked out, even to myself, that i was pregnant. i never saw a doctor. i did not tell anyone. not even my mother who i am very close to. i only gained eleven pounds in the whole pregnancy, & there was a part of me that did not believe it was real. that blocked it out. a couple of times bob asked if i was, but i denied it. just said i was gaining a little weight. he did not want to believe it, either, so i guess he didn't. i was so afraid of losing bob. i really loved him. i did not want something to spoil what we had.

"we were heading east. had stopped in idaho falls. in the middle of the night, at the motel, i went into labor. bob did not know. that's why i freed him of any charges, & took all the blame myself. grabbing the bedspread, in the dark, i crept to the bathroom & closed the door. huddled on the floor, i gave birth."

tears began streaming down her face. she hesitated. blew her nose. quietly she went on as i reached out & held her hand.

"i don't even remember everything. i was so scared. so terrified. i did not want bob to know. i could not bear losing him."

"cathy, did you have any pain medicine. anything to help you?"

"huh-uh. the baby came & i just took my panties & strangled it. oh, ann, it sounds so awful, & i cannot believe i would do such a thing. i love babies. lots of times, i have taken care of my little nephew. but i did not really know what i was doing. it did not seem as if i was killing a baby. just something i knew would ruin my life & take the one person i had opened myself to love & trust away."

i wept with her. it was clear to me how, in that small, cold, dark bathroom, it seemed rational to her. to her, it was her only option. it was beyond my comprehension how she could have delivered a normal seven-pound baby, totally alone. no support. no medicine to ease the pain. she had never been pregnant before. her first delivery.

we talked quite a while. it was surprising for me to learn that her sentencing was the next morning. there would be no trial. she had pleaded guilty.

in that narrow, impersonal corridor of the county jail, i fell in love with this young, obviously broken, shattered girl.

"oh, ann, can God really love me? it was such an awful thing i did. there is so much pain in me. so much guilt & grief."

she was not hard. not smug. not cold & indifferent. she was leveled & broken & very scared.

"yes, cathy. God loves you. He loves us regardless of anything we have ever been or done. not only does He love us, & forgive us, if we ask…but He tells us He will work *everything* for good if we love Him.

"cathy, you will never be the same. in a good & beautiful way. you might have lived a relatively mediocre life. happy with very commonplace things & feelings. less sensitive…but you can become something powerful & great as a result of all this. of recognizing your humanity. your sin. of experiencing God's love in such an extraordinary dimension." then i asked, "what is a dream you have?"

"more than anything, i still want to be a teacher. but the attorney says i will get 20 years. everything is ruined."

i looked her in the eyes. i believed. "cathy, someday you *will* be a teacher. you can take extension classes in prison.

you can grow & learn even behind bars. many people are more imprisoned, living free, than you will be. let your heart & spirit experience God's love. trust Him, moment by moment, for the things you most fear. let Him teach you & protect you. i love you, cathy. someday, you *WILL* be a teacher! hold on to that & never give up!"

i hugged her. we cried together. then prayed. & i slipped out of the jail into the cold, black night. through blinding tears, i drove to my beautiful, snug, custom-built home. checked on my baby in his colorful nursery. slipped under the covers next to my loving, strong husband.

it seemed so unfair to me. a girl whose life was really victimized by events beyond her control. young & lovely & intelligent & soft & feminine, & facing twenty years in a state prison.

thousands of women abort babies in their eighth & ninth months, & it is legal. they are cleared. understood, accepted. cathy waits. delivers. takes the baby's life seconds after birth, & she is shunned. shamed. punished for the major, key years of her youth. it just did not seem right.

i had promised to be at her sentencing. walking into the courtroom amidst waiting photographers, newsmen, etc. i noticed a small group of people huddled to one side.

walking up, i asked, "is one of you cathy's mother?"

"i am," spoke a quiet, simple woman. dignity in her voice. poise. a nurse.

"my name is ann. i met cathy last night. she told me, in spite of everything, you have really loved her. you are one of her best friends. i wanted to tell you how remarkable you are. how brave. losing a husband tragically. now nursing your paraplegic son. today, here to watch your daughter sentenced. i admire you. if there's anything i can do for you, let me know."

finding a seat in the courtroom that put me in direct eye contact with cathy. i sat down. she walked in with her attorney, & cast the warmest smile my way. pale & very frightened-looking, but poised.

one testimony after another that supported her worth & potential. had never been a delinquent. had no record. was a very strong student. the court psychologist stated she was stable, extremely bright, obviously repentant. even two jailers stood & said she had created a unique spirit of love & kindness toward other prisoners, & had been a positive force in keeping peace.

her mother took the stand. weeping. it was beyond her comprehension that her daughter would do something so awful. her brother, father of her nephew, said she had always been wonderful with their baby, & they still trusted her.

at one point, the boyfriend, seated with the family, stumbled out of the courtroom sobbing uncontrollably. i was wrenched. he had his own grief. his own shame. he was going free. yet it was his insistence on "no kids" that scared cathy into her crime. that terrified her so of losing him until the murder of the baby seemed less evil.

it was obvious the judge was moved. his voice cracked several times. he, too, mentioned something being wrong with a society that allowed over two million abortions a year...murder of the unborn...but took a young girl like cathy & crucified her. he felt obliged to punish cathy, however, & sentenced her to 18 years in prison.

the sound of the gavel. we all rose. the judge walked out. followed by cathy & the attorney.

i looked across the aisle at the tear-stained, dignified mother. she came to where i was, & threw her arms around me, & wept.

when the judge gave the sentence, i wanted to stand & cry out, "please give her to me. my husband & i would love to have her live with us. we have a baby she could help us with. let us look after her..." but i knew it was futile.

we write. cathy & i. her mother writes me. i send permissible things in the mail. some tapes. a gold cross & chain. & however long it takes, i will stand by cathy & believe that her finest hour is ahead. that someday, she *will* teach. that her life is not destroyed by one, sinful, horrible, fatal act, but because of God's love & forgiveness, enhanced. she will be stronger, purer, have more impact than otherwise imagined. that out of failure has come truth. a facing of herself. a wholeness.

i know another woman. she had read my books. one day, she bought a ticket on my same flight...arranged to have

her seat next to mine...and when i boarded, said, "hi, i'm
_____. the one who has written you for several years. this was
the only way i figured i could ever meet you."

she was very short. 280 pounds. i was exhausted from
an appearance. the last thing i wanted was to be bugged the entire flight by this strange woman.

somewhere between that one city & the next one, i
fell in love with this person. not attractive in the eyes of the
world. a prostitute. a drug addict & alcoholic. but she was real.
she wore no masks. she revealed her ugliest parts. she was not
ashamed or too proud to cry. to say she needed help. her language was rough. her stories were shocking. she was a person
needing a friend. a sinner needing a Savior.

she did not barge into my life. i rarely heard from her
until recently when she called to say she had been to an "acid"
party. went to bed with more than one man. was pregnant.

five months into her pregnancy, she miscarried. took
the bus to the hospital. waited two hours in emergency before
they looked at her. one nurse told her she deserved this because
she wasn't fit to bring a baby into the world anyway. of course,
my friend believed that. she had a history of rejection since
childhood. but it made the night so much darker to have no
kindness or compassion shown.

the baby...a perfectly formed male...would never
breathe or bring joy to the adoptive couple she had picked. his
death was just another sign of her badness. of her lack of worth.
of her nothingness.

even as i write, i am very teary & shaken. as another
woman, struggling for wholeness, i know some of the pain in
these two women's lives. no, i have never murdered a baby. or
been a prostitute or drug addict. but i have felt deeply insignificant. very afraid. inferior. ugly. unworthy. sinful. lost. i have
wondered how God could possibly love me, to say nothing of
the finite humanity around me. i certainly have had a hard time
loving myself.

until one learns to value oneself...to see the good
...the important...to forgive & let be forgiven...there can
never be wholeness.

for some of us, it takes a mighty army to bring us to the

end of ourselves. to help us fully recognize who we are *not*, & who God is. to so humble us & break us until we no longer live guarded & cautious...with clenched fists...determined to get out of life what we are SURE is right for us to demand our own way in the world. to live on our own strength.

for me, there was no deep healing...no genuine, authentic wholeness...until i relinquished all i ever hoped to be into the hands of God. gave it up. totally. until i began to believe...absolutely...that God *did* love me. that He would "withhold no good thing" from me. that i could trust Him with my life. no strings attached. only utter trust.

out of the taste of many tears, came a peace & well-being i had never before known. i began to enjoy will in a new way. to experience him as never before because i was not so wrapped up in my own pain.

others, too. they became so much more valuable to me because i had lain my own pain & uncertainty down, & was free to reach out to them in theirs.

after months...then years...of the most stubborn, brutal fighting with God over my desire for a baby, i lay the burden down. i closed the door to the still-empty nursery at the end of the hall, but closed it not in anger & grief, but suddenly with hope that something better was in store for me. with rest. with the confidence that God knew my deepest heart's desire (for a child) & i could relax & trust Him.

every now & then, i would slip into the nursery on a quiet afternoon. look at the colorful things on the walls, pull open a drawer in the "hope chest," & hold a tiny nightie. but the pain was gone. the horrible tug of "if i do not get this, i will NEVER be happy..."

wherever you are, i care. i may not fully understand *your* struggle, but i do understand *struggle*. for 39 years, i have sought, as for water in a desert, to come to a place of wholeness in my life. of peace with myself. with God. with others.

i still walk with a crooked stick, up a steep hill, looking for more.

but today there is more security & joy than ever before. it is a result of many pursuits, none as powerful as standing face-to-face with my Creator.

i stopped fighting so hard in my finite way. i internalized…& experienced…the truth that with all my crippled, wounded places, He loved me. i could trust Him.

# 15.
# *Having Fun*

## ann

"honey, why are we stopping at this sporting goods store," i asked with a frown.

"because tomorrow i am taking you fishing!"

FISHING! i had tried to like fishing. we had fished on our honeymoon & various places. with people who came to visit us in idaho. either i was too cold or too hot. the worms were so fat & wiggly & slimy & disgusting. my line always seemed to tangle with someone else's. worst of all, it seemed so boring. waiting, it seemed forever, for a fish to bite. tomorrow we had to go fishing AGAIN?

for will, it was fun. his favorite childhood memories were of his dad taking him to wild & wonderful wildernesses to fish.

the next day was warm & sunny. my mother-in-law came to watch the babies. another couple joined us. a new fishing pole was in the trunk, that will said he bought just for me. for hours, i had been praying God would help me to learn to like fishing.

it took an hour to arrive at a certain part of the snake river. parking the car in the shade, i crawled out with 5 layers of clothes on. will convinced me i could get cold, & nothing spoils my fun quicker. the men informed me we had a hike before arriving at the choice spot.

"see, honey, i thought of you. some exercises. a little workout. i knew you would like that."

the "hike" was a 1,000 foot drop, almost straight down, to the river below that looked miles away. i could not imagine staying vertical on such a drop-off. this *was* fun. i was happier by the minute. anything that involved challenge &

muscles, & was outdoors... well, i liked that.

the hike down was not nearly as hard as the steep, vertical hike back up in pouring rain & claps of thunder & lightning over our heads. we had crawled through brush to fishing holes. will was my hero & guide. salmon flies crawled on my neck & i screamed. worms wiggled off the hooks & we lost a few. i would try to cast right out to the spot will showed me. tammy caught the biggest trout of the day.

we laughed. we screamed to each other above the roar of the river. we shared worms. bob & tammy kept trying to pull my line free from places it continually snagged in the river. we cheered each other on. no airplanes. no campers. no noises but rushing water & exotic birds & a coyote way off in the distance. the smell of pine & unmarred earth. a crisp, clean breeze. pulling each other up the incredible incline, sliding in the mud as it began to rush down the cliff. driving through a tiny town en route home & passing a little baptist church, & will saying, "let's stop & see if the minister lives next door, & encourage him."

hot tea & cookies in the little trailer where the elderly couple pastor this tiny church. often only one or two others besides themselves worship there.

now THAT is what i call fun!

it did not start out sounding fun. i resisted the fishing idea. i *often* sort of balk at will's ideas for fun. but without exception, as i pull myself out of my own struggles & go along with him, we have a great time.

the last few years would have leveled me if there had not been some fun. the pregnancy problems. the miscarriages. the changes, the struggles that even a good marriage can bring. less travel. more housework. the stripping of outer securities & the little, basically weak, small, trembling seed of who i *really* was. fun moments carried me. even taking taylor, at 7 months, & going to the ice-cream stand. having will fix a seat on the back of my bike, & riding taylor around the neighborhood, listening to his cooing & gurgles.

running beside jan in a 10K race july 4. our first race together. neither of us in good shape. a last minute decision. pinning on our numbers. jumping up & down at the starting line. no pressure. tom up ahead, to run faster & stronger. the hills. the heat. the unknown course. but jan beside me. the camaraderie.

everyone waiting for us at the end. oranges & soda pop & hugs & sweat & the feeling of wonder that we did it. & in decent time, too. of feeling the rhythm & pulse in my body that only running can bring.

donuts & laughter & kids on our laps.

hot baths & shampoos & clean, dry clothes & a parade.

except that will could not be here (business meeting in chicago). july 4 has been SO FUN! oh, jan, i love you. we did it. we ran & we did not walk & we finished! yahoooo.

for me, fun is going to bed with babies tucked in to cribs after years of longing for them. it is will picking me up & carrying me to bed. the sound of the fan & the cool night air coming in off the patio, & a few hours just for me...to sleep.

will & i just returned form vacationing with tom & jan in california. we often all stayed in one big room. children. babies. adults. tom running with jan & me. will taking the kids to breakfast. ice-cream cones & surprises & ribs at my brother's. time with dad & mom. watching the baby cousins find each other.

will's grandmother, elizabeth, is in her nineties. beautiful & brilliant. she borrows books from harvard's library, in latin, not wanting to lose her touch with the language. she often told will growing up "people often go through life & never know when they are happy. it is usually a memory of the past or a hope in the future." today, right where you are, have fun.

find happiness, amidst the disappointments & the financial crunch & the overweight body & the rejection, discover the small, simple joys. create some magic. search for & find the good & the beautiful that is often hidden under layers of stress & sorrow & pain.

tom & jan's second son, nash recently spent a week with us. 5½ years old. along with my two babies, it was a lot of work. a can of pop spilled on the white carpet. a little voice always asking me, "aunt ann, what can i do now for some fun?" an extra mouth to feed. another head to shampoo.

but what fun we had. listening to nash as he took showers with will. all the giggles & screams of delight. the bathroom never knew such sounds before. the moments nash would wrap his arms around my neck.

"aunt ann, i love you. oh, aunt ann, i do. i will miss you when i go home."

pancakes & popcorn & feeling this little body crawl in bed with us in the night & snuggle close. watching him carry 2-month-old brock around, while i prayed he wouldn't drop him.

"aunt ann, i will help you baby-sit brock & taylor because i need some more money. i only got $34 in the bank." big, earnest, brown eyes flashing.

i am learning to have fun with the little obscure moments. in the most simple ways. even on blue days. in tough situations. when i am not sure where my value is, & will has had a bad potato season. without humor & a little laughter, the complexities of life would wash over me & drain all my joy & hope in an abyss of despair.

"honey, let's just pick up the babies, & get into the car, & go find someone to visit."

i suggested that one frustrating sunday afternoon, & we ended up having so much fun that now it is ritual. tradition. every sunday evening, with babies in our arms, we take ice cream or cake somewhere, & surprise people. we begin to laugh & share. our children play together. suddenly we forget all the problems facing us. the seemingly impossible dilemmas. we are not alone. there is fellowship. & with laughter, there is hope for anything.

# Jan

This morning, July 4, Ann and I ran our first race to-gether—a ten-kilometer run in Canton, Ohio. Tom was going to run it with our good friend Rick DeBlander, and Ann, in Cleve-land for only a couple of days, suggested she and I run too. You know, "Just a fun work out," she said. "I'm sure I'll have to walk part of the way, but we can talk and just make it easy." Well, that didn't sound bad at all. I was certainly up for a fun, easy work-out. I have never been a conscious competitor. I suppose all of us compete in some way and in certain moments with other people in our lives, but I can't ever remember setting out with the goal in mind to beat someone else in anything. I always grew up believing that if I tried to pass someone else up I would for sure fail and the humiliation of that would be worse than just being ordinary and unnoticed. I have, however, always tried to do my best—to compete with myself.

At the start of the race Ann and I hugged. "This is going to be fun," Ann said. While Ann has been the mara-thoner, in the last four years she has basically quit all running in her attempts to carry a pregnancy full-term. I at least am run-ning a couple of miles one to three times a week trying to rid myself of the seven pounds left over from my last pregnancy. However, this morning as we stood there, I realized it had been almost two weeks since I'd run. I was not going to worry though because Ann had been reporting to me repeatedly what horrible shape she was in. "You are going to far outdo me, and I'm afraid this is going to be boring for you," she kept saying. I relaxed—with her in this weakened condition. I wouldn't have to worry.

It was a warm morning—too warm for my comfort. During the first mile Ann was complaining that she would have been smart to just go after the two-mile fun run instead of this 6.2-mile race. I have heard her complain like this before and then just completely outrun everyone, so I was listening cautiously. At the end of the first mile, we headed into a long upgrade, and I was aware as we were running that she wasn't complaining anymore. Instead, I was annoyed as she led us past some people on our way up the hill. My breathing was heavy, and I tried to detect some sign of any stress coming from her body. She was running smooth and easy. She was feeling good—better than expected—I could tell. Clipping along, looking like my mind remembered her looking in the old days, when we would go run together and she was the heroine—the big marathon runner.

We passed the three-mile mark, and she continued carrying on a conversation with me. I blurted out, "You may talk all you want—I can't. I can't believe you're doing so well—I should have known this would happen. This always happens. But I must not get angry. Anger saps energy, and I need all I can draw out of my muscles and bones." Gasping for air I just kept moving. On the level stretches I felt only average, but I was well aware that Ann was feeling good. She had strength and endurance coming from somewhere. "God loves her more," I muttered to myself. I began to think of the deliveries of my three sons. In my mind I relived those moments in the delivery room, and the pain of the race became endurable. I knew I had developed some bad blisters. I was terribly warm and remembered Tre screaming to me during the Revco Race, "This is my last race—I mean it." I should have been more sympathetic.

As I was suffering and trying to concentrate on anything but the seeming eternity of this race, my mind began focusing on all my clients who were struggling to run their race of life.

I know they are having great questions of whether they will survive till their crisis is over. They want to quit—walk a while. Become promiscuous, drunk, irresponsible—anything except to keep doing what in the long haul is going to give them peace. My mind suddenly focused in on the words of a thirty-year-old, single, female client who confrontingly said to me, "You winced when I said life is too hard, but I'm telling you it is. I've lost two babies, grew up in an abusive home, am raising a retarded daughter with no financial help, am putting myself through college, and now have to face retaking a course I didn't feel I flunked."

"God, help her today—this moment," I began to pray, "I want to quit. This is too hard. She's having as much pain and difficulty running her race as I am right now running this one. I want to run for *her* today, God. I realize in this moment how easy it would be to quit. Take my determination to keep going and somehow use it to inspire her to not give up."

I prayed for clients. I prayed for my three little, marvelous sons and my strong, wonderful husband, Tom. I prayed and kept my body going through the motions of moving after my mind had long since lost its ability to believe this was *ever* going to be a good experience. Ann was always a couple of steps ahead of me.

At the sixth mile, I gasped out the words, "Ann, you have always been my leader—maybe that is part of the reason you're doing so well. Your follower is back by your side and struggling. Get me to the end. I need you." We both burst into tears, and Ann expressed how meaningful it was for this moment to be my leader again. Having a leader did not mean I was weaker. I felt no more anger—just desperation for someone to help me finish what I had begun to pursue. She talked me through the last half-mile, while I gagged and cried and promised myself I'd never do this again. She grabbed my hand the last few feet and dragged me across the finish line. Tom, Rich, Cathy (his wife), their three beautiful little girls, Tre with a can of pop, and Nash were there to celebrate. After a few minutes of recovery, I began to laugh and hug Ann and the children, and believe it or not began to talk about how fun this had been. Our first race together at age thirty-nine!

Having fun involves more than moments or hours of sheer bliss and peace—free from all anxiety. Sometimes having fun involves moments of short-term pain, challenge, and endurance. But it's experiencing something meaningful either alone or with someone you care about. Playing sports or climbing a mountain or doing white-water rafting can have their short-lived seconds or minutes of great intensity, fear and hard work, but they also bring the feelings of exhilaration, success, laughter, and escape from those longer lasting, more complicated, complex issues of life that fill most of our hours. You may be surprised when I tell you that sometimes doing therapy is absolutely fun to me.

Sometimes fun is doing exactly what is easy and without any challenge. I remember the wintry day I was going to be alone, so I went to the closest bookstore and bought a biography I had been wanting to read. I came home, baked a batch of cookies, and sat for hours curled up on my sofa with an afghan wrapped around me, munched cookies, and escaped into someone else's life.

When I think of having fun I think it means getting involved doing something that will bring me peace and a sense of well-being. I am actually meeting a personal need of some kind when I engage in something that is fun for me. Are you sometimes surprised by the reality that in everything we do we meet some deep need inside ourselves? Even when we do something we resent and resist doing, we are at least meeting the need to please or keep someone's approval.

When I run, I meet the need of feeling good about my body.

When I read, I feel stimulated and confirmed that I am surely smarter than what my fifth-grade experience told me I was.

When I spend an evening reading books and playing games with my children, I feel like I'm a good mother, being true to the needs of those in my care.

I can get so caught up in living and working and keeping deadlines and worrying about how I'm ever going to be good and smart and strong enough, that I fail to understand the significance of having fun. It's these great fun moments that get us through all the awful, grim, discouraging situations of life. It's the moments we really throw back our heads and laugh together uncontrollably that we are able to survive any relationship. If there is no fun between us, our bonding will disintegrate and die.

Elisabeth Kubler Ross, M.D., believes that people have the greatest difficulty dying if they have never really experienced life. Regardless of whether you are single or married, young or old—there are uncountable opportunities today everywhere around you that can bring you moments of joy, laughter, exhilaration, and stimulation. It is in these moments we find strength to face all the rest that life can deal out.

Tom, from the day I married him, has been creating what he calls "cheap fun." Recently we met some great people, Nathan, Marie, and Natalie Price, in California and spent a few days together. We reserved four dormitory rooms at a college there right on the Pacific to conserve funds. We were each handed the thinnest washcloth, hand, and bath towels you ever touched and were directed to four of the grimmest, sparsest rooms I've ever seen. No wonder college kids get depressed! We had to share a common bath and every time we flushed a toilet, the sewer backed up in the shower. The odor was almost intolerable. Every morning early, Nathan would go out and bring in hot coffee and donuts, and we would sit and laugh and solve the world's problems (our own, that is!). Tom is right—there's plenty of cheap fun for everyone to enjoy. One night the baby was asleep and Tom took one boy and I the other. We read, played games, and then Nash and I went to the kitchen and created banana splits for everyone and brought them up on a tray. Cheap, wonderful fun. Connecting with people you enjoy and adding just a touch of sparkle.

A happy memory is a joy forever!

# 16.
# *Affirmation*

## ann


affirmation. we all need it.

the last four years have so affected my confidence. it is so hard for me, today, to know how people feel about me because they do not often verbalize it.

a woman had run from jackson, wyoming, to idaho falls. 57 years old. a tough, well-conditioned athlete, especially at her age. a few women in my neighborhood had a little coffee for her, & invited me. i was delighted to be included, but with 2 babies, 11 months apart, i did not know how i could get them bathed & dressed...& myself ready...& to the baby-sitter's ...back to the neighbor's home by 10:00 A.M.

with much energy, i delivered two clean babies & bottles & diapers to the sitter's...& flew into the coffee about 5 minutes late. people asked how the children were. they were warm & gracious. the food was delectable. meeting the runner was most enjoyable. but walking out to the car, i was consumed with a sad feeling. no one had said:

"ann, i love what you are wearing."
or "ann, you look *so* wonderful..."
or "oh, you have lovely children."

the conversation was friendly & chatty, but not affirming. i had no sense of how I really looked, or what i was as a person.

another night, i left the babies with my mother-in-law, & dashed off to a private, small party. will was out of town, but everyone begged me to come anyway. i felt a little shy, being alone with all couples, but i brushed my hair. donned a white, crisp, cool, linen dress. tied a bright, wide sash around my waist,

& wanted desperately to fit in. to feel significant. again, everyone praised me for coming alone. everyone seemed genuinely delighted to see me. but i longed to hear words that never came. to have statements *handed* over about my personhood. my value. my worth.

WHY is there so little affirmation in the world? i have some ideas, but i am beginning to believe that unless i help educate those around me, i will just continue to feel more & more unsure & empty.

during the evening, at the party, we began to share around the circle. it took me a while to express what i was feeling. "this is very hard for me, but i left home tonight so needing encouragement. when i looked in the mirror, it seemed i looked fresh & vibrant. but it was just a mirror. no one this evening has made any comment about me as a person. especially in my most vulnerable, unsure areas. if there is *anything* positive you see about me, please share it. i have been home with babies all day. there is no professional circle right now that has scooped me up & is carrying me on to glory. if you think being a writer & speaker is all i need, you are wrong. i am standing at the well, hoping for any drop of water you can hand me."

there were tears in my eyes.

i felt naked & silly & weak & puny.

affirmation can change the worst day into something decent & lovely. everything can go wrong, but i can fly into the grocery store to get a carton of milk, & have someone say, "ann, you're looking wonderful," & suddenly the whole world seems better.

we were eating brunch at a beautiful chalet in sun valley. will & i & some dear friends. i kept watching the table across from ours. a family. they were animated. laughing. their spirit of camaraderie could be felt even where i was sitting. when we left, i slipped over & tapped the mother on the shoulder. they all turned toward me. "i have been enjoying your togetherness over at my table. you exude such warmth & love that those around you can feel it. it seemed important that i stop & just say 'thank you.' " their faces were radiant.

will & i were in the gigantic anaheim stadium at a convention. a beautiful woman was walking toward us, on her way to the next balcony. i tapped her arm. "you are a beautiful lady," i smiled. her whole face lit up. a split second. a passing in the crowd. just a few words. i believe it touched her life.

there is a friend who always makes me feel very welcome at her home when i am speaking in her city. her husband & children are loving. she fixes fantastic meals. she tells me i am like family. the bed is freshly made. we munch popcorn in our robes around the t.v. & laugh & visit. every time i am there, though, a sinking, sad feeling takes over. i never *really* know how she values me.

i try to rave about her clothes (which really *are* sharp). i brag about her husband & children. over & over, i tell her she's one of my favorite cooks. always, i try to be honest. to not fake anything. but to keep looking for positives that i can, with clear conscience, feed back into her.

she came to hear me address 4,000 women. now, i know how simple & uncomplicated my speeches are, but i needed some input from her, no matter what it was. it was one of those blessed moments when the air was charged. there was electric magnetism between the audience & myself. God had really anointed me.

the standing ovation was loud & long. several thousand women stood in line to shake my hand. to seek an autograph. all that was very reassuring, but it was my friend, the only one in the entire audience that i felt really close to, that mattered to me. she hugged me. she said she was thrilled to see me. she did not even mention the speech. maybe it shouldn't have, but it mattered to me. i longed to hear something. *ignoring* it ...saying *nothing*...hurt more than if she had made a negative comment.

did she feel so negative about my speech that she chose silence over honesty with me? was there NOTHING she could find good to comment on? was she jealous, & so unsure that she could not reach beyond her own pain to where i was?

every chance i get, i try to affirm my little sons & husband. with specifics.

"brock, you have the most beautiful brown eyes."

"taylor, i was so proud of you yesterday, when you did not cry & you played by yourself."

"honey, i like that shirt. you look sharp."

"will, you are a terrific father."

we are too busy in our own little struggles. our own insecurities. too caught up with living to give those around us a moment of praise. you may say i am too dependent & wrapped up in other people's opinions. that it should not matter. that i am narcissistic. maybe so. you can *never* convince me, however, that the world would not have more ego strength & there would be more joy dancing around…more confidence…more courage …if one could learn to verbalize more of the positives that we think & feel about others.

a pretty dress. flawless skin. an impeccably dressed man in the elevator. a little girl with new barrettes. a little boy's idea. someone's beautiful, new home. the neighbor's new car…or yard. *everywhere* there are things that deserve praise. verbal celebration.

& all the while, we sit around like hungry beggars. longing for reassurance of our value. waiting. starving.

jan taught 3rd grade once. a long time ago. one bright-eyed boy would stand at her desk. watch her. talk to her. all the while wrapping his finger around a piece of her hair into a little curl. he thought jan was the shining star in the night. over & over, however, he did poorly in his work assignments & daily quizzes.

one day jan stopped, looked at him, & said, "rodney, you are very smart. you could be doing so well in school. in fact, you are one of my finest students…" before she could continue to tell him that he should be doing much better in school…he looked up at her with sober, large eyes:

"i did not know that!"

from that moment on, rodney began to change. his papers were neater. cleaner. his spelling improved. because he was one of her top students. all because she affirmed him. she told him something no one ever had before. it changed his life.

there are thousands of readers who are fans of my writings, & through the years have written me letters of love & support. without them, i would have evaporated into a nothing state. into a person with little concept of my worth. the people who are often the closest to me never let me know. i spend a lot of time feeling my clothes are defective. feeling i look very below par. knowing i must be rather blah & limited. without jan, & will (who is learning), i would have no happy, healthy concept of my value. if i receive such little affirmation, where does that leave the rest of the world? surely i am not that much more defective than anyone else.

once, after lunch, i confessed these feelings to a friend.

"ann, you always seem so self-assured! probably none of us feel you need anything from us." what a tragic reason to not verbalize something positive...that is honest...to someone who is human, & thus always will need reassurance & support.

please...join me. every time you see a happy child, praise him for his sunshine. every time you think a beautiful thought about someone, express it to them in words. if with every human being we encounter...in an elevator, across a store counter, in a restaurant, at a party...we could look for & find one lovely, beautiful quality, & *VERBALIZE* it, there would be a new level of productivity. fresh, creative energy. a joy & confidence that the world has not, as yet, experienced.

i will not become cocky with too much praise. i will never leave you out of my life because i feel more valuable. instead, there will be more love for you because you have given me worth, & freedom to reach beyond myself & my own flaws. all the positive, admiring thoughts in the world will *never* generate a magical, wonderful moment unless they are spoken. shared.

one quiet, honest statement of praise to human beings can change them.

today, running across the street...downtown...after having my driver's license renewed...a lady passed me.

"what a beautiful outfit you are wearing!" she yelled across the wind.

i stopped. overwhelmed. smiled widely.

"what a lovely, kind, wonderful thing to say," i responded.

one simple woman. one beautiful statement. & i was changed.

# Jan

After observing at the private school my children formerly attended, Tom and I met with two of their teachers. I had an issue to bring to the table.

"My children have been attending here now for several months, and I've observed your classrooms on different occasions. There is one aspect of your system that is bothering me. I have never heard you express any personal statements of affirmation to my children nor to any of the others. I have listened to hear you say, 'My, Nash—that is a wonderful picture you have drawn,' or 'Tre, I feel you did an exceptional job on your book report.' "

One of the teachers was ready with a quick response, obviously anxious to inform me on the *why* of this. "No, and you never will," she replied firmly. "We find that the most insecure children are those who have received a lot of external affirmation and are always looking to an adult figure to affirm them before they seemingly are able to move on to another project independently. We rather like to make statements like, 'My, Nash, you must be proud of how hard you have worked on that picture,' and 'My, Tre, you really must be pleased with the way your book report turned out.'

"We want these children to learn how to affirm themselves and become more self-directed as opposed to externally directed."

Now this is the other side of the coin of what Ann just spoke to—that of being affirmed by others. I see it over and over again as a therapist—this tremendous need for each of us to learn how to affirm ourselves.

162

I am reminded of my adviser, one of my major professors, in graduate school. In her closing statements to me she said, "You have some tremendous skills and strengths for being a wonderful therapist. There is just one thing I want to comment on. Therapy can be very lonely, and there may be days and weeks when you won't receive much feedback from your clients about your work. You are a person who underestimates your own value and who is unsure of yourself. You tend to look to and be dependent on external sources to assure you of your strengths. You are going to have to learn to support and reinforce yourself more, or you may end up very discouraged. You must begin to believe that you are good at what you do."

I said to a client today, "Tell me three things about yourself that are positive and strong." She is beautiful, brilliant, charming, and social, but she sat there and said, "I can't." "You *won't*," I retorted. Facing and acknowledging my own strengths is a part of my facing reality. The fact that I am still alive makes a statement to my belief that there is something—even just one thing—I believe to be of merit in myself or I would have died long ago.

However, practicing self-support can never be enough. It will never eliminate nor devalue the great healing power and encouragement I will receive from your verbal affirmation.

I really must have both. Too much self-support and too little need and appreciation for your support will keep me from the love and insights that only you can give me. On the other hand, very little belief in myself leaves me almost totally dependent on you and makes it impossible for me to survive without you. I have to keep remembering that when you affirm me, however, you are simply reporting your individual perspective—not the entire world's nor necessarily the absolute truth. But in that moment in time, your loving words to me, genuinely spoken, can alter my behavior and perhaps my life if I will hear and respond to them.

As children, most of what Ann and I received from our peers was negative. I can tell you that I concluded early in life that those negatives must represent the truth and nothing but the truth. I wasn't mature enough to realize that those negative comments represented only a small fraction of how a poll of a thousand individuals would have responded. A very brilliant, young, male client of mine finishing up his Ph.D. in biochemistry said to me, "I was overwhelmed last week at my farewell party by the loving and kind words of the people I have worked with. I find myself still believing more the feedback I received as an eighth and ninth grader." Someday, if he can keep hearing positive affirmation, maybe he will be able to rebuild his self-concept.

Affirmation that is wrapped up in specifics and not generalities is the most powerful. "I love you." "I'm glad to see you." "We have a lot in common," can apply to many different friends. I remember the day I turned to Tom after we had been married about three months and with deep feelings said, "Honey, I so love you." He looked at me and winked and said, "Why?" *Why?* Well I hadn't really thought about why. But it is in the *whys* I realize now that we are able to influence people's concepts of themselves.

My father, whenever he stood by me in church and could hear me sing, would comment on my "beautiful" voice. I grew up feeling proud of my voice and always am confident joining a church choir. Affirmation that tends to be directed at specific attributes often gives me the confidence I need to develop that part of me further. I have a couple of clients who are models and in the fashion business. They keep telling me I have a creative flair with clothes. With their affirmation I find myself much more confident to tie a sash a unique way or wrap something around my neck that normally goes around a bedspread. I march out of the house with a new internal belief that maybe I am creative.

I don't even need someone standing at the door every moment to reinforce my decision. See, the more you are willing to express your positive response to some part of me you believe to be unique and beautiful, the more I can stand on my own—keep developing and improving that part of me and become more self-directed. The ones of you who are free to affirm me—to point out to me where you see I am strong—are the people who are really responsible for helping me become who I am today. Telling me you love me is important, but not nearly as important as words that point out some beauty in me I cannot see and maybe never will. As a therapist I know that there is a part of me I can *never* see, regardless of how much introspection I pursue, unless you show it to me. I am blinded to parts of myself and desperately need you to reveal them to me—and then to remind me of them *again*. Telling someone once that you admire their ability to be clever must be said again and again. Sometimes it takes a few times before I am able to really hear and believe you. And if we are growing individually and together, we will discover new and different beautiful pieces of each other to affirm. It's endless. Please keep telling me so I can keep growing and become more able to believe in myself.

I will never forget the night not long ago, that Ann said, "If I could look as good as you I would be willing to gain ten pounds." I've had a baby in the last year and for the first time in years and years, I weigh more than Ann. I've struggled with this. To hear Ann, who I have desperately always wanted to be "as good as" share with me that she wants to be like me, was a moment of deep healing for me. I closed my eyes feeling I must be beautiful and worthwhile if Ann wanted to look like I did.

Your children, husband, next-door neighbor, mother, father, are waiting to hear some beautiful thing about themselves. People will do a lot of things in a desperate attempt to hear someone say something affirming to them. I had a very attractive, young woman come to see me depressed and unsure of herself. "I need help with my obsession of spending money. I go shopping when I'm depressed and buy hundreds of dollars worth of clothes. I'm desperately trying to gain approval, but nobody tells me I look good anyway, so it doesn't really help."

Look around you today and begin to find the beauty and strength in those you see. Don't keep these thoughts to yourself. Beautiful thoughts—unspoken, unexpressed verbally—are lost treasures. Give them away. Tap someone on the arm and remind them that you believe they have worth and you will find you are giving a gift to yourself as well. The Bible says, "Give and it will be given to you" (Luke 6:38). When we are kind, we give the gift back to ourselves.

And if there is a person in your life you need to hear some affirming words from—*ask.* "John, can you tell me three things you liked about me when you married me?" or "What part of my personality do you enjoy the most?"

Remember:

1. As you observe the people who will pass through your life today, look for the unusual, and use words to give away your thoughts.
2. Give yourself at least one compliment and visualize in your mind a picture of how you would like to look or behave.
3. Be willing to *ask* for what you need. This is a sign of becoming a responsible adult.

Ann was being very *adult* when she opened up to the group that night, becoming vulnerable, in order to get a need she had met.

Play the words you receive that are affirming over and over again in your thoughts. They can be useful even years after they are heard. Sit and think a moment of some of the positive statements that have come your way.

I remember driving along in the car with Tre on his sixth birthday. I began to tell him about the day he was born. "Tre, I will never forget the day you were born. After hours of great struggle, because delivering a baby is *hard work,* you came into the world. You didn't scream or cry like most newborns. You just lay on my tummy and looked all around. You never closed your eyes. Dr. Adams repeatedly told us what a beautiful baby you were. And when they took you down to the nursery to wash you up and dress you, you were still looking all around—quietly."

Tre was absorbed with my words, and when I was done, he smiled and said, "Mommy, I just loved that story. Tell it to me all over again."

When someone affirms you, don't treat it like a non-important message you read and throw in the trash. Carry it with you. Repeat it over and over again in your mind. When someone sends me a note full of beautiful thoughts they have of me, I carry it in my purse for days. I read and reread it. Those words are great treasures that restore my soul, straighten my shoulders, and put laughter in my life.

Ann, you are absolutely right when you say that "affirmers are world changers." I want to be one!

# Closing

On September 22, 1985, Ann and I turned forty. As the day approached I found myself anxious—concerned that someone might feel obligated to throw a big surprise party for me. That seemed to be the procedure for the event. I found myself distraught at the very thought of being the one in the limelight and causing so much inconvenience to "someone" who would feel obligated to throw a party. My next thought, however, was to imagine no one doing anything, confirming how very insignificant my forty years of living must have been (except, perhaps, to my mother). And that thought was more nerve-racking than the first.

I crawled into bed next to Tom one night after a week or two of worry and concern and said, "Honey—what would you think if I said I want to throw my own birthday party?"

His eyebrows went up and he smiled a strange smile. "That would certainly be different," he replied.

"Honey, I'm serious—I've just had an inspiration. I want to invite twenty-five to thirty women in this city who have touched my life in a special way. There are three things I'm going to ask for.

"First, I want them each to bring me one of the books that have meant the most to them. I love to read, and I can't think of anything I'd rather have than some new reading material.

"Second, I want them to write on the flyleaf two statements of affirmation about me. What could mean more to me as I move into middle age?

"And third, I want them to add one piece of advice." I was bounding with excitement and internal confirmation that this was the answer to my birthday dilemma.

I composed a letter and had my secretary make thirty copies. I catered a very simple luncheon at a dear friend's, whose large home can accommodate such an occasion. Ann was able to come also—she made a stop in Cleveland on her way home from a speaking tour.

The morning of the party I awoke in a state of shock. What in the world had I done? What a bizarre idea. I began to think, *Not only will I be the focal point of attention, but I've asked for it, which is a bit presumptuous from almost anyone's perspective.* I had gone too far, however, to reverse my plans.

We dressed and headed for Kay's home. I greeted each of my marvelous guests at the door with a hug and took my wrapped book. I was overwhelmed by their excitement and joy at being invited. You would have thought I had done them a favor. The scene was a far cry from the years in my childhood when I waited along the playground fence for someone to find me unique and special enough to reach out to.

I can't put into words what happened in that room that day. It really was a love feast between me and each one of those women who had so touched my heart and life in the past few months and years. We laughed and cried and hugged and celebrated each other. God came. It was like nothing I had ever experienced before. Many of the women said it was the greatest party they had ever been to. I drove home that day believing I could survive any experience in life so long as those women and God were on my side.

I'm so thankful Ann and I have traveled forty years down this journey called life. "When I was a child I talked as a child, I understood as a child, I thought as a child; but when I became a [woman], I put away childish things" (1 Corinthians 13:11). We've laid down a lot of childish ways and moved beyond many of our childish understandings of life through forty years of experience. I used to just react to people and situations I encountered. Today I understand things so much more clearly— how complex life really is. There are no simple problems.

Early in my adult life I used to find myself angry, judgmental, and combative. Like a child, I found it easy to put the blame elsewhere. Today I have a much kinder, softer heart. I can even allow others to disagree with me and not see them as an adversary.

I remember when Ann was confident and convinced

she could quickly find the answer to any dilemma. Today she is cautious about giving a solution to someone who asks. Children want and expect immediate responses to their needs. As mature adults, we learn that the best can only come to us through process and time.

Recently Tom took me, our three sons, and boths sets of our parents to Hawaii for ten days. The land of my childhood. Only my second trip back in twenty-five years. I was consciously aware of how different my thoughts were from those I had when we were there three years previous. I was made aware once more that I really can grow and change if I determine to work at it. I must *daily* choose growth over stagnation—reality over fantasy—healthy ways of responding to life's circumstances, as opposed to unhealthy, sick responses such as blame, laziness, and apathy.

The Royal Hawaiian Hotel is a big, pink castle right on Waikiki Beach. It is the old, exclusive hotel that used to stand out on the beach and now is nestled down among dozens of high-rise hotels and condominiums. When Ann and I were children our parents took every tourist from the mainland to the Royal Hawaiian to walk through the lavish lobby and see the huge, fresh flower arrangements. When we were sixteen and seventeen years of age, we baby-sat at the Royal. People would leave their children with us and head for the hotel's famous Monarch Room for dinner and the show. I remember the night Ann had a job thirty minutes before mine. I was sitting in the lobby waiting to go up to my assigned room when a rather distraught couple walked up to me and accusingly said, "We just left you upstairs with our children and what in the world are you doing sitting down here?"

As as child, I fantasized many times about spending a night in the Royal. After our trip to Oahu three years ago I told Tom, "I don't want to come back unless I can spend one night at the Royal Hawaiian." Tom banked that in his memory and made reservations for just him and me to spend that one night on this trip.

At a few minutes before 7:00 P.M. we walked up to the desk to check in. Our parents and children were staying down the street. I felt like I was going on my honeymoon. The gentleman behind the desk asked when we were checking out, consulted his computer, then looked at us and said, "I'm going to give you an upgrade on your room. I'm going to give you the $850 a night suite overlooking the ocean. It's a great room. Have a wonderful night."

I could scarcely believe my ears. Could he be serious? "Sir, you couldn't possibly understand the significance of this. Over thirty years ago I grew up here in Oahu. At sixteen years of age I baby-say in this hotel. As a child, my fantasy was to grow up and to spend a night in the Royal. This is that night. Sir, only God could have orchestrated this."

Excitedly we went up to our suite, the finest place in the house, I'm quite sure. A living room, dining room, TV room, and two private bedrooms and baths. We went down to the Monarch Room for dinner and were seated right next to the stage. I began to cry. This was a Cinderella story—a night etched out by God to remind me that dreams really can come true—that life is full of surprises and hope. My father was right: It pays to follow God. We called and had my parents bring Tre and Nash to stay in the other bedroom. I felt completely whole. I fell in love with Tom Ream all over again that night.

The years between my childhood and that night in the Royal Hawaiian Hotel represent thousands of experiences. Out of some of my greatest failures have come my greatest successes, and out of my deepest hurts have come some of my strongest beliefs.

Ann and I have always tried to take what life handed us and learn from it. We've been teachable. We've let weeks and months and years of positive and negative experiences teach us—enhance us—mellow us and reform us. They have led us to God and truth, to compassion and tenderness.

The thrill of that night was a reality only because I had struggled through and risen above thirty years of life's experiences. This process is what wholeness is about.

It is 10:30 P.M. and the house is quiet. Tre and Nash are bedded down for the night in self-made forts in the living room. I've just finished rocking Christian, now sixteen months old, back to sleep after a coughing spell. Tom is studying for a class he will be teaching at the church tomorrow. It seems like yesterday when Ann and I landed in Jackson Hole with two very young infants on that bitter cold winter night and began to pen the first lines for this book. Now, ten months down the road, Lila, our editor, is waiting for this Closing. The rest of the book, including the pictures, are ready to be sent to press. Since that first night in Jackson Hole, Ann has miscarried the twins she was pregnant with, but six weeks later adopted a second beautiful baby boy they named Brock. We have both experienced more success and defeat. Tonight we are still struggling, but we are achieving integration inside ourselves of who we are and who God is and what life is all about. Peace and serenity are becoming closer friends.

I think we are learning that the solution to this inner struggle is not to pool all our energies and go out and conquer life. We are not equal to that challenge. Life is unpredictable—often brutal. Somewhere down the road it will hand us staggering challenges that will leave us struggling to survive. Rather, we must open up our hearts and minds to what great lessons life can teach us. We must become vulnerable; learn how to surrender—how to let go of what we have or are fighting for so we can find something greater. Ann and I and you are here not for the purpose of great achievement, accumulated success, or wealth. We are here to be broken and remolded. Our celebration must be not in what we have achieved but in who we have become.

Yes, Ann and I choose this path of struggle, for it is leading us deeper into the true meaning and significance of life. Life may be harder at moments, but it's also better than it has ever been. Wherever you are—don't give up your struggle for more wholeness. Someday we will all get to the top of a mountain and look back and understand how it fits together. And how much more beautiful and serene the view will be from the top of the mountain.

JAN KIEMEL REAM